PIRLS 2016
Assessment Framework

2nd Edition

Ina V.S. Mullis
Michael O. Martin, Editors

TIMSS & PIRLS
International Study Center
Lynch School of Education, Boston College

Copyright © 2015 International Association for the Evaluation of
Educational Achievement (IEA)
PIRLS 2016 Assessment Framework, 2nd Edition
Ina V.S. Mullis and Michael O. Martin, Editors

Publishers: TIMSS & PIRLS International Study Center,
Lynch School of Education, Boston College
and
International Association for the Evaluation of Educational Achievement (IEA)

Library of Congress Catalog Card Number: 2015931452
ISBN: 978-1-889938-28-8

For more information about PIRLS contact:
TIMSS & PIRLS International Study Center
Lynch School of Education
Boston College
Chestnut Hill, MA 02467
United States

tel: +1-617-552-1600
fax: +1-617-552-1203
e-mail: pirls@bc.edu
pirls.bc.edu

Boston College is an equal opportunity, affirmative action employer.
Printed and bound in the United States.

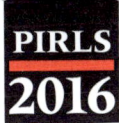

INTRODUCTION … 3

PIRLS 2016—Monitoring Trends in Reading Literacy Achievement … 3

History of the PIRLS, PIRLS Literacy, and ePIRLS International Assessments … 4

Updating the PIRLS 2016 Framework for Assessing Reading Achievement … 6

Policy Relevant Data about the Contexts for Learning to Read … 7

Using PIRLS Data for Educational Improvement … 8

Chapter 1
PIRLS 2016 READING FRAMEWORK … 11

Ina V.S. Mullis, Michael O. Martin, and Marian Sainsbury

A Definition of Reading Literacy … 11

Overview of the PIRLS Framework for Assessing Reading Achievement … 13

PIRLS Framework Emphases in PIRLS, PIRLS Literacy, and ePIRLS … 14

Purposes for Reading … 15

Processes of Comprehension … 18

Introducing ePIRLS—An Assessment of Online Informational Reading … 22

ePIRLS—Assessing the PIRLS Comprehension Processes in the Context of Online Informational Reading … 24

Selecting PIRLS and PIRLS Literacy Passages and ePIRLS Online Texts … 27

PIRLS 2016 ASSESSMENT FRAMEWORK, 2ND EDITION

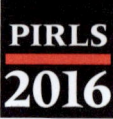

Chapter 2
PIRLS 2016 CONTEXT QUESTIONNAIRE FRAMEWORK ... 31
Martin Hooper, Ina V.S. Mullis, and Michael O. Martin

Home Contexts ... 36

School Contexts ... 40

Classroom Contexts ... 45

Student Characteristics and Attitudes Toward Learning ... 51

Chapter 3
ASSESSMENT DESIGN FOR PIRLS, PIRLS LITERACY, AND ePIRLS IN 2016 ... 55
Michael O. Martin, Ina V.S. Mullis, and Pierre Foy

Student Population Assessed ... 55

Reporting Reading Achievement ... 56

PIRLS and PIRLS Literacy Booklet Design ... 58

Question Types and Scoring Procedures ... 62

Releasing Assessment Materials to the Public ... 65

ePIRLS 2016 Design ... 65

Context Questionnaires and the PIRLS 2016 Encyclopedia ... 67

REFERENCES ... 71

Appendix A
ACKNOWLEDGEMENTS ... 89

Appendix B
SAMPLE PIRLS PASSAGES, QUESTIONS, AND SCORING GUIDES ... 99

Appendix C
SAMPLE PIRLS LITERACY PASSAGES, QUESTIONS, AND SCORING GUIDES ... 141

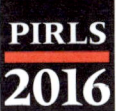

Introduction

PIRLS 2016—Monitoring Trends in Reading Literacy Achievement

Because developing reading literacy ability is vital to every student's growth and maturation, the International Association for the Evaluation of Educational Achievement, more widely known as IEA, has been conducting regular international assessments of reading literacy and the factors associated with its acquisition in countries around the world for more than 50 years.

IEA is an independent international cooperative of national research institutions and government agencies that has been conducting studies of cross-national achievement since 1959. IEA pioneered international comparative assessment of educational achievement in the 1960s to gain a deeper understanding of policy effects across countries' different systems of education.

PIRLS (Progress in International Reading Literacy Study) was inaugurated in 2001 as a follow-up to IEA's 1991 Reading Literacy Study. Conducted every five years, PIRLS assesses the reading achievement of young students in their fourth year of schooling—an important transition point in children's development as readers. Typically, at this point in their schooling, students have learned how to read and are now reading to learn. PIRLS is designed to complement IEA's TIMSS assessments of mathematics and science at the fourth grade.

PIRLS 2016 is the fourth assessment in the current trend series, following PIRLS 2001, 2006, and 2011. Over 60 countries and sub-national, benchmarking entities are participating in PIRLS 2016, including many that have participated in previous assessment cycles since 2001. For countries with data since 2001, PIRLS 2016 will provide the fourth in a series of trend measures collected over 15 years. These countries will have the opportunity to evaluate progress in reading achievement across four time points: 2001, 2006, 2011, and 2016.

Since its inception, PIRLS has been a collaborative effort among the participating countries and IEA. PIRLS is directed by the TIMSS & PIRLS International Study Center at Boston College in close cooperation with the IEA Secretariat in Amsterdam and IEA's Data Processing and Research Center in Hamburg. Statistics Canada monitors and implements sampling activities, the National Foundation for Educational Research (NFER) in England and the Australian Council for Educational Research (ACER) provide support for item development, and Educational Testing Service consults on psychometrics.

History of the PIRLS, PIRLS Literacy, and ePIRLS International Assessments

The number of countries participating in PIRLS has grown with each assessment cycle. All of the countries, institutions, and agencies involved in successive PIRLS assessments have worked collaboratively to improve PIRLS and build the most comprehensive and innovative measure of reading comprehension possible.

Participants have worked equally hard to provide information about the educational contexts for learning to read in each country so that PIRLS data are an extremely useful resource for policy relevant information about improving reading achievement. PIRLS always has included school, teacher, and student questionnaires, and PIRLS 2001 pioneered the Learning to Read Survey, completed by students' parents or caregivers, as well as the PIRLS Encyclopedia, comprised of chapters written by each participating country describing its reading curriculum and instruction.

In 2006, PIRLS was expanded to report results by comprehension processes in addition to literary and informational reading purposes. Also, greater emphasis was given to the PIRLS Curriculum Questionnaire completed by each participating country.

In 2011, the PIRLS and TIMSS assessment cycles came together, providing a unique opportunity for countries to collect reading, mathematics, and science achievement data on the same fourth grade students. Also in 2011, IEA broadened PIRLS to meet the needs of countries in which most children in the fourth grade are still developing fundamental reading skills. For example, if students are more likely to have developed the reading comprehension competencies necessary for success on PIRLS by the fifth or sixth grade, IEA began encouraging participation in PIRLS at those grades. Additionally, IEA provided a less difficult version of the PIRLS reading assessment for fourth grade students (called prePIRLS). The international results for the PIRLS 2011 assessments were published in two reports: *PIRLS 2011 International Results in Reading* (Mullis, Martin, Foy, & Drucker, 2013) and *TIMSS and PIRLS 2011: Relationships Among Reading, Mathematics, and Science Achievement at the Fourth Grade—Implications For Early Learning* (Martin & Mullis, 2013).

PIRLS 2016 represents the most significant changes in PIRLS to date, because it encompasses two new assessments of reading comprehension, PIRLS Literacy and ePIRLS, which are described in the following sections.

PIRLS Literacy

The PIRLS Literacy assessment is equivalent to PIRLS in scope and reflects the same conception of reading as PIRLS, except it is less difficult overall. PIRLS Literacy 2016 includes some passages and items that also are included in PIRLS 2016, but most of the assessment is based on shorter passages with higher proportions of more straightforward questions.

The purpose of the PIRLS Literacy assessment is to provide better measurement at the lower end of the scale. Countries whose fourth grade students are still developing fundamental reading skills can participate in the PIRLS Literacy assessment and still have their results reported on the PIRLS achievement scale. The reading passages and questions in common between the PIRLS Literacy and the PIRLS assessments will enable the two assessments to be linked, so that the PIRLS Literacy assessment results can be reported together with the PIRLS assessment results and directly compared to them (for details, see Chapter 3).

Depending on a country's educational development and the students' reading level, countries can participate in either or both PIRLS and PIRLS Literacy. One approach would be to participate in PIRLS Literacy at the fourth grade and PIRLS at the sixth grade. The goal is to provide the best policy-relevant information about how to improve teaching and learning and to help young students become accomplished and self-sufficient readers.

ePIRLS

ePIRLS is an innovative assessment of online reading, designed to be responsive to the information age and provide important information about how well students are developing 21st century skills. Internet reading increasingly is becoming one of the central ways students are acquiring information (Leu, Kinzer, Coiro, Castek, & Henry, 2013; Leu, O'Byrne, Zawilinski, McVerry, & Everett-Cacopardo, 2009; Murnane, Sawhill, & Snow, 2012). The Internet also is becoming the central source for students to gather additional information in their school subjects, such as science and social studies. As students have begun to rely on the Internet, reading curricula around the world are beginning to emphasize the importance of developing online reading skills and competencies such as reading for information (see *PIRLS 2011 Encyclopedia*).

For countries participating in PIRLS 2016, ePIRLS expands PIRLS to include computer-based reading assessment. ePIRLS uses an engaging, simulated Internet environment to present fourth grade students with authentic school-like assignments involving science and social studies topics. An Internet browser window provides students with websites containing information about their assignments, and students navigate through pages with a variety of features, such as photos, graphics, multiple tabs, and links. In an assessment window, a teacher avatar guides students through the ePIRLS assignments, prompting the students with questions about the online information. The development of the ePIRLS approach to assessing online reading benefited greatly from the work of ORCA (the Online Reading Comprehension Assessment), where students research science issues in an online environment (see Leu, Kulikowiich, Sedansk, & Coiro, 2008).

Updating the PIRLS 2016 Framework for Assessing Reading Achievement

Based on reading purposes and comprehension processes, the PIRLS framework provides the foundation for the PIRLS, PIRLS Literacy, and ePIRLS assessments of students' reading achievement.

PIRLS assesses students' reading achievement within the two overarching purposes for reading that account for most of the reading done by young students both in and out of school:

- Reading for literary experience; and
- Reading to acquire and use information.

The PIRLS assessments integrate four types of comprehension processes within each of the two purposes for reading:

- Focus on and retrieve explicitly stated information;
- Make straightforward inferences;
- Interpret and integrate ideas and information; and
- Evaluate and critique content and textual elements.

Updating the PIRLS framework with each assessment cycle provides participating countries opportunities to introduce fresh ideas and current information about curricula, standards, frameworks, and instruction. This keeps the frameworks educationally relevant, creates coherence from assessment to assessment, and permits the framework, instruments, and procedures to evolve gradually into the future.

For PIRLS 2016, the framework was updated using information provided by the National Research Coordinators (NRCs) from the participating countries in the *PIRLS 2011 Encyclopedia* (Mullis, Martin, Minnich, Drucker, & Ragan, 2012). In addition, the PIRLS 2016 reading expert committee (Reading Development Group) provided direction. Using an iterative process, the framework, under the direction of the committee, was once again reviewed by the NRCs and updated a final time prior to publication.

Policy Relevant Data about the Contexts for Learning to Read

In order to provide an important context for interpreting the reading achievement results, PIRLS collects considerable background information about how educational opportunities are provided to students as well as the factors that influence how students use these opportunities. These background data include information about the following: national curriculum policies in reading and how the educational system is organized to facilitate learning; students' home environment for learning; school climate and resources; and how instruction actually occurs in classrooms (see Chapter 2).

The PIRLS Encyclopedia has been published with each assessment cycle since 2001. Each PIRLS country prepares a chapter summarizing the structure of its education system, the language and reading curriculum in the primary grades, and overall policies related to reading instruction (e.g., teacher education, instructional materials, and assessment). The *PIRLS 2011 Encyclopedia* is a valuable compendium of information about how reading is taught around the world and provides an indispensable resource for policy and research in comparative education.

In order to obtain the background information that is published together with the PIRLS achievement results, PIRLS asks students, their parents, their teachers, and their school principals to complete questionnaires about their home, school, and classroom contexts for learning to read. In particular, the Learning to Read Survey, completed by students' parents and caregivers, has been an important component of each assessment cycle of PIRLS since 2001. It provides valuable information about students' home support for early literacy learning and reading experiences. Also, the student questionnaire contains a series of questions about students' behaviors and attitudes toward reading literacy, because these are an important part of lifelong reading and contribute to the full realization of the individual's potential within a literate society (Organisation for Economic Cooperation and Development, 1995; 1997; 2000; 2005; 2010).

The upcoming PIRLS 2016 assessment will collect and report data on a variety of activities and experiences from the following range of learning to read contexts:

- National and community;
- Home;
- School;
- Classroom; and
- Student.

As a result, the assessments will provide a dynamic picture of reading educational policies and practices across the participating countries that can raise issues and indicate avenues relevant to educational improvement efforts.

Using PIRLS Data for Educational Improvement

As reported in the *PIRLS 2011 Encyclopedia*, countries use PIRLS data for system-level monitoring of education achievement in a global context. They compare their reading achievement levels and contexts for learning with those of other countries, and monitor progress in reading achievement over time. Many countries reported initiating educational reforms when PIRLS achievement results were low compared to other countries, or lower than expected. That is, many countries also view the PIRLS results in the context of national goals.

Working to achieve equity provided another impetus for reform and a number of countries reported having made special efforts to reduce achievement disparities among ethnic, social, or regional groups. Countries implementing educational changes typically look to future PIRLS assessment cycles to monitor improvement.

PIRLS data, framework, released items, and scoring guides often are used as a basis for updating curriculum and textbooks, as well as for improving classroom instruction, primarily through teacher workshops and training programs. Many countries reported increased sponsorship of reading research activity, including research using PIRLS data, and several have established national reading centers.

Introduced for the current TIMSS assessment cycle, TIMSS 2015 also includes a new, less difficult mathematics assessment called TIMSS Numeracy. Together, PIRLS Literacy and TIMSS Numeracy are intended to be responsive to the needs of the global education community and can support efforts that work toward universal primary education. As debates shift from *access* for all to *learning* for all, both assessments can provide a much-needed means for countries and international organizations to effectively measure and thereby improve reading and mathematics learning outcomes for young students worldwide.

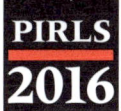

CHAPTER 1

PIRLS 2016 Reading Framework

Ina V.S. Mullis, Michael O. Martin, and Marian Sainsbury

The PIRLS 2016 Reading Framework and the instruments developed to assess this framework reflect IEA's commitment to be forward thinking and incorporate the latest approaches to measuring the reading achievement of young students in their fourth year of schooling. PIRLS is based on the broad notion of what the ability to read means—a notion that includes the ability to reflect on written texts and to use these texts as tools for attaining individual and societal goals, also known as "reading to do" (Stiggins, 1982). This view is increasingly relevant in today's society, where greater emphasis continues to be placed on students' ability to use the information they gain from reading (Organisation for Economic Cooperation and Development, 1995; 1997; 2000; 2001; 2005; 2010). Emphasis is shifting from demonstrating fluency and basic comprehension to demonstrating the ability to apply what is read to new situations or projects (Coulombe, Trembly, & Marchand, 2004; Smith, Mikulecky, Kibby, & Dreher, 2000; see also *PIRLS 2011 Encyclopedia*).

The PIRLS framework for assessing reading achievement was initially developed for the first assessment in 2001, using IEA's 1991 Reading Literacy Study (Elley, 1992; 1994; Wolf, 1995) as the basis for the PIRLS definition of reading literacy and for establishing the aspects of reading comprehension to be assessed. Since then, the PIRLS assessment framework has been updated for each subsequent assessment cycle (Campbell, Kelly, Mullis, Martin, & Sainsbury, 2001; Mullis, Kennedy, Martin, & Sainsbury, 2006; Mullis, Martin, Kennedy, Trong, & Sainsbury, 2009).

A Definition of Reading Literacy

The PIRLS definition of reading literacy is grounded in IEA's 1991 study, in which reading literacy was defined as "the ability to understand and use those written language forms required by society and/or valued by the individual."

With successive assessments, this definition has been elaborated so that it retains its applicability to readers of all ages and a broad range of written language forms, yet makes explicit reference to aspects of the reading experience of young students as they become proficient readers, highlights the widespread importance of reading in school and everyday life, and acknowledges the increasing variety of texts in today's technological world. Currently, the PIRLS definition of reading literacy is as follows:

> Reading literacy is the ability to understand and use those written language forms required by society and/or valued by the individual. Readers can construct meaning from texts in a variety of forms. They read to learn, to participate in communities of readers in school and everyday life, and for enjoyment.

This view of reading reflects numerous theories of reading literacy as a constructive and interactive process (Anderson & Pearson, 1984; Chall, 1983; Kintsch, 1998; 2012; 2013; Ruddell & Unrau, 2004; Rumelhart, 1985). Meaning is constructed through the interaction between reader and text in the context of a particular reading experience (Britt, Goldman, & Rouet, 2012; Snow, 2002). Readers are regarded as actively constructing meaning as well as knowing effective reading strategies and how to reflect on reading (Afflerbach & Cho, 2009; Langer, 2011).

Before, during, and after reading, readers use a repertoire of linguistic skills, cognitive and metacognitive strategies, as well as background knowledge to construct meaning (Baker & Beall, 2009; Kintsch, 2012; 2013; Pressley & Gaskins, 2006; Rapp & van den Broek, 2005). In addition, the context of the reading situation can support the construction of meaning by promoting engagement and motivation to read, but the context also can place specific demands that might not support the construction of meaning (Christianson & Luke, 2011; Lorch, Lemarie, & Grant, 2011; Miller & Faircloth, 2009; Taboada, Tonks, Wigfield, & Guthrie, 2009).

In order to acquire knowledge of the world and themselves, readers can learn from a host of text types. Any given text type can take many forms and combinations of forms. These include traditional written forms, such as books, magazines, documents, and newspapers, as well as digital forms such as email, text messaging, and Internet websites where text often is integrated with various multimedia formats (Leu, Kinzer, Coiro, & Cammack, 2004; Leu, Kinzer, Coiro, Castek, & Henry, 2013; Rosell & Pahl, 2010; Reuda, 2013).

Throughout the framework, various sources that have provided a research and scholarly basis for the framework are referenced. These references are only a sample of the volumes of literature and research that have informed the PIRLS framework, including considerable research by countries participating in PIRLS.

Discussing what they have read with different groups of individuals allows young students to construct text meaning in a variety of contexts (Almasi & Garas-York, 2009; Murphy, Wilkinson, Soter, Hennessey, & Alexander, 2009). Social interactions about reading in one or more communities of readers can be instrumental in helping young students gain an understanding and appreciation of texts (Galda & Beach, 2001; Kucer, 2005). Socially constructed environments in the classroom or school library can give young students formal and informal opportunities to broaden their perspectives about texts and to see reading as a shared experience with their classmates and teachers (Alvermann & Moje, 2013; Guthrie, 1996). This can be extended to communities outside of school as young students talk with their families and friends about ideas and information acquired from reading.

Overview of the PIRLS Framework for Assessing Reading Achievement

Based on reading purposes and comprehension processes, the PIRLS framework provides the foundation for the PIRLS assessment of students' reading achievement in their fourth year of schooling, as well as for PIRLS Literacy, a literacy assessment that is an easier version of PIRLS, and ePIRLS, which extends PIRLS to assess online reading. As shown in Exhibit 1, the PIRLS framework focuses on the two overarching purposes for reading that account for most of the reading done by young students both in and out of school: for literary experience, and to acquire and use information. In addition, the PIRLS assessment integrates four broad-based comprehension processes within each of the two purposes for reading: focus on and retrieve explicitly stated information, make straightforward inferences, interpret and integrate ideas and information, and evaluate and critique content and textual elements.

Exhibit 1: The PIRLS Reading Purposes and Comprehension Processes

Purposes for Reading
Literary Experience
Acquire and Use Information

Processes of Comprehension
Focus on and Retrieve Explicitly Stated Information
Make Straightforward Inferences
Interpret and Integrate Ideas and Information
Evaluate and Critique Content and Textual Elements

It should be acknowledged that the purposes for reading and the processes of comprehension do not function in isolation from one another or from the context in which students live and learn.

PIRLS Framework Emphases in PIRLS, PIRLS Literacy, and ePIRLS

Although the two reading purposes and four comprehension processes form the basis for assessing PIRLS as well as PIRLS Literacy and ePIRLS, there are some differences in emphases across the assessments. Exhibit 2 presents the reading purposes and processes assessed by PIRLS and the percentages of the test devoted to each for PIRLS, PIRLS Literacy, and ePIRLS.

Exhibit 2: Percentages of the PIRLS, PIRLS Literacy, and ePIRLS Reading Assessments Devoted to Each Reading Purpose and Comprehension Process

	PIRLS	PIRLS Literacy	ePIRLS
Purposes for Reading			
Literary Experience	50%	50%	0%
Acquire and Use Information	50%	50%	100%
Processes of Comprehension			
Focus on and Retrieve Explicitly Stated Information	20%	50%	20%
Make Straightforward Inferences	30%	25%	30%
Interpret and Integrate Ideas and Information	30%	25%	30%
Evaluate and Critique Content and Textual Elements	20%		20%

Both PIRLS and PIRLS Literacy devote half of the assessment passages to each of the purposes for reading, while the ePIRLS online assessment focuses solely on reading to acquire and use information. The ePIRLS approach simulates websites from the Internet, through which students can navigate to accomplish school-based research projects or tasks. Because PIRLS Literacy is designed for students earlier in the process of learning to read, a larger percentage of items (50 percent of the assessment) are devoted to measuring foundational reading comprehension processes—the ability to focus on and retrieve explicitly stated information. Also, PIRLS Literacy has shorter reading passages with easier vocabulary and syntax.

Purposes for Reading

Throughout the world, reading literacy is directly related to the reasons people read; broadly, these reasons include reading for pleasure and personal interest, learning, and participation in society. The early reading of most young students centers on the first two reasons, and thus often includes reading of narrative texts that tell a story (e.g., storybooks or picture books) or informational texts that tell students about the world around them and answer questions. As young students develop their literacy abilities and are increasingly required to read in order to learn across the curriculum, reading to acquire information from books and other print materials becomes more important (Duke, 2004; Duke & Carlisle, 2011; Palincsar & Duke, 2004; Wharton-McDonald & Swiger, 2009).

Aligned with these reading purposes, both the PIRLS and PIRLS Literacy assessments focus on reading for interest or pleasure and reading to learn—that is, reading for literary experience and reading to acquire and use information. Because both purposes for reading are important for young students, the PIRLS and PIRLS Literacy assessments contain an equal proportion of material assessing each purpose. However, because much online reading is done for the purpose of acquiring information, ePIRLS specifically focuses on reading to acquire and use information.

The PIRLS and PIRLS Literacy assessment passages are classified by their primary purposes, and the accompanying questions address these purposes for reading. That is, passages classified as literary have questions addressing theme, plot events, characters, and setting, and those classified as informational are accompanied by questions about the information contained in the passages. Although the assessments distinguish between purposes for reading, the comprehension processes readers use are more similar than different for both purposes; therefore, the comprehension processes are evaluated across all passages, including the ePIRLS Internet-like texts.

Each purpose for reading often is associated with certain types of texts. For example, reading for literary experience often is accomplished through reading fiction, while reading to acquire and use information generally is associated with informative articles and instructional texts. However, the purposes for reading do not align strictly with text types. For example, biographies or autobiographies can be primarily informational or literary, but include characteristics of both purposes.

Texts often differ in the way in which ideas are organized and presented, eliciting a variety of ways to construct meaning (Goldman & Rakestraw, 2000; Kobayashi, 2002). Text organization and format can vary to a great degree, ranging from sequential ordering of written material to snippets of words and phrases arranged with pictorial and tabular data. The content, organization, and style that may be typical of a particular text genre have implications for the reader's approach to understanding the text (Alexander & Jetton, 2000; Graesser, Golding, & Long, 1996; Lorch, Lemarie, & Grant, 2011; Weaver & Kintsch, 1996).

As noted, it is in the interaction between reader and text that meanings are constructed and purposes are achieved. In selecting texts for the PIRLS assessments, the aim is to present a wide range of text types within each purpose for reading. The goal is to create a reading experience for students participating in each assessment that, as much as possible, is similar to authentic reading experiences they may have in and outside of school.

Reading for Literary Experience

In literary reading, readers engage with the text to become involved in events, settings, actions, consequences, characters, atmosphere, feelings, and ideas, and to enjoy language itself. In order to understand and appreciate literature, each reader must bring to the text his or her own experiences, feelings, appreciation of language, and knowledge of literary forms. For young readers, literature can offer the opportunity to explore situations and feelings they have not yet encountered.

Events, actions, and consequences depicted in narrative fiction allow readers to experience vicariously and reflect upon situations that, although they may be imagined, illuminate those of real life. The text may present the perspective of the narrator or a principal character, and a more complex text may even have several viewpoints. Information and ideas may be described directly or through dialogue and events. Short stories or novels sometimes narrate events chronologically, or sometimes make more complex use of time with flashbacks or time shifts.

The main form of literary texts used in the PIRLS and PIRLS Literacy assessments is narrative fiction. Given differences in curricula and cultures across the participating countries, it is difficult for PIRLS to include some forms of literary texts. For example, poetry is difficult to translate and plays are not widely taught in the primary grades.

Reading to Acquire and Use Information

Informational texts are both read and written for a wide variety of functions. While the primary function of informational text is to provide information, writers often address their subject matter with different objectives. Many informational texts are straightforward presentations of facts, such as biographical details or steps to accomplish a task; however, some informational texts are subjective. For example, authors may elect to convey facts and explanations through an expository summary, a persuasive essay, or a balanced argument. A reader must bring to these texts a critical mind in forming his or her own opinion.

In order to best address the various functions of texts, information can be presented differently, such as by varying the content, organization, and form. Young students may read informational texts that cover a range of content, including those that are scientific, historical, geographical, or social. These texts also may vary in the organization of the content conveyed. For example, historical facts may be organized chronologically, instructions or procedures sequenced step-by-step, and an argument presented logically (e.g., cause and effect, or compare and contrast).

Information can be presented in many different formats. Even informational pieces that are primarily presented via text may include a table to document facts or a picture to illustrate a description. Both print materials (e.g., manuals and newspapers) and websites present a considerable amount of information via lists, charts, graphs, and diagrams. In addition, words need not be in the form of continuous text, such as in advertisements or announcements, or in sidebars to the text that offer supplemental information such as definitions, lists, or timelines. As noted, different presentations of textual content can demand that readers apply different comprehension processes. Finally, it also should be emphasized that a piece of informational text often incorporates one or more methods of presenting information.

The informational texts used in the PIRLS assessments reflect students' authentic experiences with reading informational text in and out of school. Typically, these passages, as well as some of the ePIRLS websites, have been written by authors who understand writing for a young audience, and are provided by the participating countries as representative of the informational materials their students read.

Processes of Comprehension

Readers construct meaning in different ways. Therefore, PIRLS assesses four broad-based processes of comprehension typically used by fourth grade readers: focus on and retrieve explicitly stated information; make straightforward inferences; interpret and integrate ideas and information; and evaluate and critique content and textual elements. Transcending these processes are the metacognitive processes and strategies that allow readers to examine their understanding and adjust their approach (Baker & Beall, 2009; Kintsch & Kintsch, 2005; Paris, Wasik, & Turner, 1996; Perfetti, Landi, & Oakhill, 2005; Pressley, 2002; vanDijk & Kintsch, 1983). In addition, the knowledge and background experiences that readers bring to reading equip them with an understanding of language, texts, and the world, through which they filter their comprehension of the material (Alexander & Jetton, 2000; Beach & Hynds, 1996; Galda & Beach, 2001; Kintsch, 2012; 2013; Wolfe & Goldman, 2005).

In the PIRLS assessments, the four comprehension processes are used as a foundation for developing the comprehension questions which are based on each reading passage (or set of passages). Across each assessment, the variety of questions measuring the range of comprehension processes enables students to demonstrate a range of abilities and skills in constructing meaning from written texts. Along with each process and its components, examples of questions that may be used to assess that process are discussed.

In thinking about assessment questions, there is, of course, a substantial interaction between the length and complexity of the text and the sophistication of the comprehension processes required. Initially, it may seem that locating and extracting explicitly stated information would be less difficult than, for example, making interpretations across an entire text and integrating those with external ideas and experiences. However, all texts are not equal and can vary with regard to length, syntactic complexity, abstractness of ideas, and organizational structure. Thus, the nature of the text can impact the difficulty of the question asked, across and within the four types of comprehension processes.

Focus on and Retrieve Explicitly Stated Information

Readers vary the attention they give to explicitly stated information in the text (Flavell & Wellman, 1977; Schneider & Pressley, 1997). Some ideas in the text may elicit particular focus and others may not. For example, readers may focus on ideas that confirm or contradict predictions they have made about the text's meaning or that relate to their general purpose for reading. In addition, readers often need to retrieve information explicitly stated in the text to answer a question they bring to the reading task, or to check their developing understanding of some aspect of the text's meaning.

In focusing on and retrieving explicitly stated information, readers use various ways to locate and understand content that is relevant to the question posed. Typically, this type of text processing requires the reader to focus on the text at the word, phrase, and sentence level in order to construct meaning (Perfetti, 2007; Perfetti & Adolf, 2012). The process also may require the reader to focus on and retrieve pieces of information from several locations.

Successful retrieval requires a fairly immediate or automatic understanding of the text (West & Stanovich, 2000). This process needs little or no inferring or interpreting—the meaning is evident and stated in the text. The reader must, however, recognize the relevance of the information or idea in relation to the information sought.

Reading tasks that may exemplify this type of text processing include the following:

- Identifying information that is relevant to the specific goal of reading;
- Looking for specific ideas;
- Searching for definitions of words or phrases;
- Identifying the setting of a story (e.g., time and place); and
- Finding the topic sentence or main idea (when explicitly stated).

Make Straightforward Inferences

As readers construct meaning from text, they make inferences about ideas or information not explicitly stated (Zwaan & Singer, 2003). Making inferences allows readers to move beyond the surface of texts and to resolve the gaps in meaning that often occur in texts. Some of these inferences are straightforward in that they are based primarily on information that is contained in the text—readers may merely need to connect two or more ideas or pieces of information. The ideas themselves may be explicitly stated, but the connection between them is not, and thus must be inferred. Furthermore, despite the inference not being explicitly stated in the text, the meaning of the text remains relatively clear.

Skilled readers often make these kinds of inferences automatically (West & Stanovich, 2000). They may immediately connect two or more pieces of information, recognizing a relationship even though it is not stated in the text.

In many cases, the author has constructed a text to lead readers to an obvious or straightforward inference. For example, the actions of a character across the story may clearly point to a particular character trait, and most readers would arrive at the same conclusion about that character's personality or viewpoint.

With this type of processing, readers typically focus on more than just word-, phrase-, or sentence-level meaning. While the focus may be on local meaning residing within one part of the text, the focus also may be on a more global meaning, representing the whole text. In addition, some straightforward inferences may require readers to connect local and global meanings.

Reading tasks that may exemplify this type of text processing include the following:

- Inferring that one event caused another event;
- Concluding what is the main point made by a series of arguments;
- Identifying generalizations made in the text; and
- Describing the relationship between two characters.

Interpret and Integrate Ideas and Information

As with the more straightforward inferences, readers who are engaged in interpreting and integrating ideas and information in text may focus on local or global meanings, or may relate details to overall themes and ideas. In any case, these readers are making sense of the author's intent and developing a more complete understanding of the entire text.

As readers interpret and integrate, they are attempting to construct a more specific or more complete understanding of the text by integrating personal knowledge and experience with meaning that resides within the text. For example, readers may draw on experience to infer a character's underlying motive or to construct a mental image of the information conveyed. They often need to draw on their understanding of the world, as well as their background knowledge and experiences, more than they do for straightforward inferences.

As readers engage in this interpretive process, they are making connections that are not only implicit, but that may be open to some interpretation based on their own perspective. Because of this, meaning that is constructed through interpreting and integrating ideas and information is likely to vary among readers, depending upon the experiences and knowledge they bring to the reading task.

Reading tasks that may exemplify this type of text processing include the following:

- Discerning the overall message or theme of a text;
- Considering an alternative to actions of characters;
- Comparing and contrasting text information;
- Inferring a story's mood or tone; and
- Interpreting a real-world application of text information.

Evaluate and Critique Content and Textual Elements

As readers evaluate the content and elements of a text, the focus shifts from constructing meaning to critically considering the text itself. Readers engaged in this process step back from a text in order to examine and critique it.

The text content, or meaning, may be evaluated and critiqued from a personal perspective or with an objective view. This process may require readers to make a justified judgment, drawing on their interpretations and weighing their understanding of the text against their understanding of the world—rejecting, accepting, or remaining neutral to the text's representation. For example, readers may counter or confirm claims made in the text or make comparisons with ideas and information found in other sources.

In evaluating and critiquing elements of text structure and language, readers draw upon their knowledge of language usage, presentational features, and general or genre-specific features of texts. The text is considered as a way to convey ideas, feelings, and information.

Readers may reflect on the author's language choices and devices for conveying meaning and judge their adequacy. Relying on their understanding of language conventions, readers may find weaknesses in how the text was written or recognize the successful use of the author's craft. Further, readers may evaluate the mode used to impart information—both visual and textual features—and explain their functions (e.g., text boxes, pictures, or tables). In evaluating the organization of a text, readers draw upon their knowledge of text genre and structure. The extent of past reading experience and familiarity with the language are essential to each piece of this process.

Reading tasks that may exemplify this type of text processing include the following:

- Judging the completeness or clarity of information in the text;
- Evaluating the likelihood that the events described could really happen;
- Evaluating how likely an author's argument would be to change what people think and do;
- Judging how well the title of the text reflects the main theme;
- Describing the effect of language features, such as metaphors or tone; and
- Determining an author's perspective on the central topic.

Introducing ePIRLS—An Assessment of Online Informational Reading

A new extension of PIRLS offered for the first time in 2016, ePIRLS is an innovative assessment of online reading that was developed in response to the explosion of information availability on the Internet. As previously described, ePIRLS is a computer-based assessment focusing on the informational reading purpose and designed to assess fourth grade students' ability to use the Internet in a school context.

Particularly relevant to the PIRLS assessment, Internet reading is increasingly becoming a key component of school curricula and one of the central ways students are acquiring information (Leu, Kinzer, Coiro, Castek, & Henry, 2013; Leu, O'Byrne, Zawilinski, McVerry, & Everett-Cacopardo, 2009; Murnane, Sawhill, & Snow, 2012; Pew Research Center, 2012; 2013a; 2013b; Rowsell, Kress, Pahl, & Street, 2013; Tondeur, van Braak, & Valcke, 2007). New digital literacies are necessary to be a successful reader on the Internet, where a successful reader is one that can meet his or her reading goals by efficiently finding and comprehending the target information (Afflerbach & Cho, 2009; Bawden, 2008; Coiro & Kennedy, 2011; Leu, Kinzer, Coiro, Castek, & Henry, 2013; Leu, Kulikowich, Sedansk, & Coiro, 2008).

Essentially, reading for informational purposes on the Internet requires all of the reading comprehension skills and strategies assessed by PIRLS, but in a different environment containing much more information. Because of the complexity of the Internet, online reading involves being able to use reading comprehension skills and strategies in contexts that are very different from those encountered in reading traditional printed materials as regularly assessed by PIRLS (Britt & Rouet, 2012; Leu, Kinzer, Coiro, Castek, & Henry, 2013).

ePIRLS focuses on the reading skills and strategies needed to derive meaning from the variety of differing presentations of online text. For example, Internet web pages appear different than typical printed pages. Although much of the Internet is devoted to providing information of one type or another, online presentations often use text sparingly. Similar to printed texts, web pages can present information in various forms, such as photos, illustrations, graphs, charts, tables, maps, and timelines. However, web pages also tend to be multi-modal in the ways they present information and contain interactive, experiential features that are not possible to reproduce in a print format. For example, online text presentations typically integrate the following dynamic elements for visual interest or illustration: videos and audio clips; animated graphics; pop-up windows with information that only appears by clicking, "hovering" above, or "rolling over" it; and a variety of code-based features, such as information that appears and disappears, revolves, or changes color.

The Internet also is a network of texts that are distributed across multiple websites and pages in a non-linear fashion. Looking for and learning information from the Internet involves comprehension of information arranged within this complex reading environment. While traditional printed text usually is read in a linear fashion, online reading consists of searching through a network of multiple texts where readers are responsible for creating their own paths. Readers first must access the appropriate website, and then use navigation strategies (e.g., multiple navigation and sub-navigation menus, tabs, and links) to move efficiently within and across one web page or site to the next.

A fundamental component of successful Internet research and comprehension, therefore, is the ability to locate information that meets one's needs. Readers need to be able to find and select the websites that will provide the target information, to navigate to the relevant web pages, and also to follow links to new websites. This may involve self-regulatory processes to maintain focus on the task at hand, so as not to be distracted by other interesting topics or advertising.

Further, Internet searches for information require the additional comprehension demands of inferring the potential usefulness of yet unseen texts (e.g., when evaluating search engine results or links). In order to begin the search for information, online readers must choose among websites to find the one most likely to contain the target information. Once on a given website or page, readers must continue to infer the relevance of the various types of information and texts presented, while ignoring a barrage of advertising.

ePIRLS—Assessing the PIRLS Comprehension Processes in the Context of Online Informational Reading

ePIRLS recognizes that online reading comprehension tasks require a blending of new digital literacies with traditional offline (i.e., print) reading comprehension processes as currently defined and assessed by PIRLS. Overall, the reading comprehension skills and strategies assessed in ePIRLS will parallel those assessed in PIRLS, with the distinction that the ePIRLS reading tasks are situated in a simulated Internet environment.

The goal of ePIRLS is to assess students' reading achievement when the notion of the PIRLS passages is greatly expanded to include a series of interconnected web pages with many different kinds of visual information, such as photos, graphs, charts, and maps, in addition to dynamic features such as videos, animations, links, and pop-up windows. The websites look very different from the typical PIRLS passages, and involve navigating between pages and sites.

The approach is based on using websites from the actual Internet as the basis for creating a closed Internet environment, through which fourth grade students can accomplish an online study of a science or social studies topic, similar to the types of projects or reports they might be asked to complete for school. Each task involves students working across approximately three different websites totaling about five to ten web pages, each containing a variety of textual presentations and visual displays, and including a variety of approaches to web navigation.

In its simulated environment, ePIRLS incorporates a set of navigation skills and strategies specifically required to locate and use information on the Internet. These include the following:

- Selecting websites that meet a particular information need; and
- Using online features to locate information within websites (e.g., content tabs, navigation bars, graphic icons, links, and scroll bars).

However, while ePIRLS is designed to simulate an authentic online reading experience, it is within a computer-based environment suitable to fourth grade reading levels and a timed assessment. In addition, although it is intended to reflect the types of online reading that students are asked to do as part of school-based projects, reports, and research assignments, the online environment of the ePIRLS assessment is necessarily very limited in comparison to the entire world of the Internet.

While recognizing that being able to locate Internet information underlies all of the reading processes, the emphasis in ePIRLS is on assessing reading comprehension rather than navigation skills. Because students have a range of Internet experiences, ePIRLS begins with a brief set of directions that covers how to click on tabs and links as well as how to scroll, when necessary. Also, throughout the assessment, the teacher avatar points students toward particular websites and provides additional assistance when students have difficulty locating particular web pages. Students that have difficulty finding the correct web pages are automatically moved along to the pages by the teacher avatar after a certain amount of time, and this information is tracked by the ePIRLS computer-based assessment. Using the device of the teacher avatar, the ePIRLS assessment moves students through the web pages so that students have the opportunity to accomplish the reading tasks in the allotted assessment time.

Focus on and Retrieve Explicitly Stated Information

In reading a printed, linear text to retrieve specific information, the text is likely to be initially read and processed at a micro-level, focusing on individual phrases or sentences. In contrast, using online sources and search strategies can involve initial macro-processing. Readers need strategies for identifying the portion of the web page that contains the important information before they can focus on the sentence, phrase, or part of the graphic that has the information.

Online reading tasks that may exemplify this type of text processing include the following:

- Identifying the part of the web page that contains the information;
- Identifying the explicitly stated information related to a specific reading goal; and
- Identifying specific information on a graphic (e.g., graph, table, or map).

Make Straightforward Inferences

As explained previously, as readers construct meaning from text, they make inferences about ideas or information not explicitly stated. Online reading requires a considerable amount of inferencing, beginning with identifying those websites most likely to have the information of interest. Next, readers need

to process the information on a web page, making connections and inferring ideas or information not explicitly stated. Readers also may infer whether it is necessary or useful to follow a link to another page.

Online reading tasks that may exemplify this type of text processing include the following:

- Choosing among possible websites to identify the most appropriate, applicable, or useful one;
- Filtering the content of a web page for relevance to the topic;
- Summarizing the main intent of a web page;
- Describing the relationship between text and graphic(s); and
- Inferring the potential usefulness of links.

Interpret and Integrate Ideas and Information

Using the Internet requires the ability to read and digest information from multiple online sources. Integrating and synthesizing information across texts is very challenging, even offline, because readers need to comprehend not only one text, but consolidate information across two or more texts. In the Internet environment, this includes information presented via animation and videos as well as in pop-up windows and rollover text and graphics.

Online reading tasks that may exemplify this type of text processing include the following:

- Comparing and contrasting information presented within and across websites;
- Relating the information in one web page or site to information in another web page or site;
- Generalizing from information presented within and across web pages or sites;
- Relating details from different web pages to an overall theme; and
- Drawing conclusions from information presented in multiple websites.

Evaluate and Critique Content and Textual Elements

The skills required to evaluate and critique online texts in ePIRLS are very similar to those required for printed passages in PIRLS. However, because anyone can publish anything on the Internet, readers also must make judgments about the credibility of the source of the information as well as determine the perspective, point of view, and bias in the text. In addition, the visual and textual features on the Internet tend to be much more varied.

Online reading tasks that may exemplify this type of text processing include the following:

- Critiquing the ease of finding information on a website;
- Evaluating how likely the information would be to change what people think;
- Describing the effect of the graphic elements on the website;
- Determining the point of view or bias of the website; and
- Judging the credibility of the information on the website.

Selecting PIRLS and PIRLS Literacy Passages and ePIRLS Online Texts

The PIRLS and PIRLS Literacy reading passages, as well as the ePIRLS online reading texts, undergo extensive review by the Reading Development Group and the National Research Coordinators. Considerable effort is expended to ensure that the texts have the following characteristics:

- Clarity and coherence;
- Appropriate content across countries and cultures;
- Interesting, engaging content for a wide range of students; and
- Adequate basis for assessing the full range of comprehension processes.

In order to reflect the goal of approximating an authentic reading experience in the assessment, the reading passages and online materials presented to students must be typical of those read by students in their everyday experiences and reflect students' authentic reading experiences, in and outside of school. In order to help achieve this goal, the texts are provided by the participating countries as representative of the literary and informational materials their students read. Texts that exist for students to read in and outside of school are more likely to reflect students' ongoing reading activities and challenges than those written specifically for a test.

The time constraints of the test situation place some limits on the length of texts, because students need time to read the entire passage and answer comprehension questions. Consistent with the difference in difficulty between

PIRLS and PIRLS Literacy, the passages for PIRLS generally average about 800 words and those for PIRLS Literacy about 400 words. However, length will vary somewhat because other text characteristics also affect rate of reading.

As an additional feature to help students locate information within the text, items in the PIRLS Literacy booklets are interspersed throughout each passage. When possible, items that require students to focus on a particular page of text are placed on the facing page, so that students can view both the items and the relevant text simultaneously. This distribution of items also helps to ensure that students can provide answers to some questions, even if they do not complete the entire passage.

The ePIRLS online informational reading tasks in science or social studies are adapted from Internet websites. As described previously, each task involves approximately three different websites totaling about five to ten web pages. Reflecting the fact that online reading often involves sorting through more information than is actually necessary to achieve one's goal, the texts contained in an ePIRLS assessment task average about 1000 words in total.

Clarity and coherence are essential criteria for PIRLS texts. Typically, the passages and websites have been written by successful authors who understand writing for a young audience, such that the texts have an appropriate level of linguistic features and density of information. In the context of an international study, attaining authenticity in assessment reading experience may be somewhat constrained by the need to translate the texts into numerous languages. Thus, care is taken to choose texts that can be translated without loss of clarity in meaning, or in potential for student engagement.

In selecting texts for use in international reading assessment, it is crucial to pay close attention to the potential for cultural bias. Texts that depend heavily on culture-specific knowledge are automatically excluded. Text selection thus involves collecting and considering texts from as many of the participating countries as possible. The goal is for the texts to be universally applicable across cultures, and for the set of texts in the assessment to range as widely as possible across nations and cultures, such that no country or culture is overrepresented in the assessment texts. The final selection of texts is based, in part, on the national and cultural representation of the entire set of assessment texts.

The appropriateness and readability of texts for the PIRLS assessments primarily is determined through iterative reviews by educators and curriculum specialists from countries participating in the assessments. Taking into account fairness and sensitivity to gender, racial, ethnic, and religious considerations, every effort is made to select texts that are topic and theme appropriate for the grade level and that elicit the full range of comprehension processes.

Finally, it is extremely important for the texts to be interesting to the greatest number of students. As part of the field test, students routinely are asked how well they like each of the texts, and a high level of positive response is fundamental for a text to be selected for PIRLS.

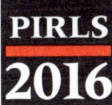

CHAPTER 2

PIRLS 2016 Context Questionnaire Framework

Martin Hooper, Ina V.S. Mullis, and Michael O. Martin

PIRLS collects extensive information about the home and school contexts for learning to read, providing educational policy makers important insights into how educational systems can be improved to foster reading achievement. The PIRLS 2016 Context Questionnaire Framework establishes the foundation for the background information collected through the context questionnaires and the *PIRLS 2016 Encyclopedia*.

In order to collect the PIRLS background information, all students participating in PIRLS/PIRLS Literacy and their parents, teachers, and principals complete questionnaires to provide data about the students' home and school contexts for learning to read. Students also participating in ePIRLS complete a short supplementary questionnaire that focuses on student computer use. In addition, representatives from participating countries complete a curriculum questionnaire and contribute a chapter to the *PIRLS 2016 Encyclopedia*. The curriculum questionnaire and *PIRLS 2016 Encyclopedia* entries provide important information on each country's educational policy, reading curriculum, and other national contexts that shape reading instruction and student learning. Chapter 3 provides an overview of the procedures for collecting background information.

The context questionnaires that accompany the reading assessment are an essential component of PIRLS data collection. The questionnaires cover a wide array of policy-relevant information about the country's various contexts for teaching and learning reading. The data on home supports for learning as well as on educational system structure, school organization, curricula, teacher education, and classroom practices are considered in relation to student achievement and compared across countries. This information can provide insight into effective educational strategies for development and improvement.

Students in the fourth year of schooling typically have gained most of their reading skills at school and at home. Community, school, classroom, and home environments that support each other can create extremely effective climates for learning. In order to reflect this situation, the PIRLS 2016 Context Questionnaire Framework encompasses five broad areas:

- National and community contexts;
- Home contexts;
- School contexts;
- Classroom contexts; and
- Student characteristics and attitudes toward learning.

National and Community Contexts

Cultural, social, political, and economic factors all contribute to the backdrop of a student's literacy acquisition. At the national and community level, key educational policy decisions are made about how best to implement the curriculum, given these contextual factors. The success a country has in providing effective reading instruction depends on a number of interrelated national characteristics and decisions:

- Language(s) and emphasis on literacy;
- Economic resources, population demographics, and geographic characteristics;
- Organization and structure of the educational system;
- Student flow;
- Reading curriculum in the primary grades;
- Teachers and teacher education; and
- Monitoring curriculum implementation.

Language(s) and Emphasis on Literacy

The historical background of language and literacy in a country can influence the challenges and instructional practices in teaching students to read. For example, some countries have one commonly spoken language, while others are historically multilingual. Immigration also can increase language diversity.

Multilingual countries across the world have different policies for educating their population. Thus, decisions about the language(s) of instruction and how to implement those decisions can be very complicated. Studies consistently have shown a learning gap associated with students who do not speak the language of instruction in the home (Entorf & Minoiu, 2005; Schnepf, 2007; Trong, 2009).

Economic Resources, Population Demographics, and Geographic Characteristics

A country's economic resources, demographic characteristics, and geographic characteristics can have a tremendous impact on the relative ease or difficulty of promoting literacy.

- **Economic Resources**—Countries have different levels of wealth and vary in how that wealth is distributed. At the national level, economic resources and socioeconomic equity tend to be linked to favorable contexts for fostering student achievement. Having economic resources enables better educational facilities and a greater number of well-trained teachers and administrators. Financial resources also provide the opportunity to invest in education through widespread community programs and by making materials and technology more readily available in classrooms.

- **Population Demographics**—The size and diversity of a country's population can increase the challenges involved in curriculum implementation. Some countries have a diversity of ethnic groups, cultures, and languages, and immigration movements can add to the diversity of the population. The curriculum and the educational system must be flexible enough to foster literacy acquisition for this heterogeneous population.

- **Geographic Characteristics**—The sheer size of a country can pose challenges to curriculum implementation. This is especially true if part of the population is isolated in remote parts of the country.

Organization and Structure of the Educational System

Some countries have highly centralized educational systems in which most policy-related decisions are made at the national or regional level. In these systems, often there is a great deal of educational uniformity in terms of curriculum, textbooks, and general policies. Other countries have more decentralized systems in which many important decisions are delegated to local governments and schools. This decentralized structure results in greater variation in how schools operate and how students are taught. Research has found that the level of centralization of standardized assessments tends to be associated with greater educational equality (Van de Werfhorst & Mijs, 2010) and higher student outcomes (Bishop & Wößmann, 2004; Jürges, Schneider, & Büchel, 2005).

Student Flow

Student flow refers to how students in an educational system progress through school. For PIRLS 2016, the student flow themes that are highly relevant include preprimary education, age of entry, the prevalence of grade retention, and student grouping.

- **Preprimary Education**—Even before they begin formal primary school, children may receive considerable exposure to literacy as part of their preprimary educational experience. As described in the *PIRLS 2011 Encyclopedia* (Mullis, Martin, Minnich, Drucker, & Ragan, 2012), countries vary dramatically in their policies and practices with regard to early (preprimary) education. PIRLS 2011 supported research findings indicating that preprimary school can have a positive effect on academic achievement during primary school (Berlinski, Galiani, & Gertler, 2009; Tucker-Drob, 2012), with longer duration of preprimary education associated with higher achievement (Sammons et al., 2002).

- **Age of Entry**—Policies about the age of entry to formal education (first year of primary school, ISCED Level 1) are important for understanding the variation in students' ages across countries at the fourth grade (Martin, Mullis, & Foy, 2011), as are policies concerning promotion/retention (see below). Typically across the PIRLS countries, students enter school at ages 5 to 7. Students entering school at older ages may have an advantage at the fourth grade for several reasons. For example, they have had the opportunity for more years of preprimary education than those students beginning school at younger ages. Also, they may have had the opportunity for more reading instruction upon beginning the first grade of primary school because they are more mature and able to cope with the complex cognitive demands of reading instruction.

- **Grade Retention**—Grade retention practices differ among countries. This variation has been explained as an effect of differing educational policies, cultural norms, and diverging perspectives on the advantages of holding students back (Goos et al., 2013). Because PIRLS is a grade-based study, the degree of grade retention can be an important factor to consider when evaluating achievement results. Research has shown that grade retention does not have a positive relationship with student achievement or the emotional wellbeing of the student (Hattie, 2009; Jimerson, 2001).

- **Grouping for Reading Instruction**—Generally, small-group instruction can improve reading ability (Lou, Abrami, & Spence, 2000; Puzio & Colby, 2010). For example, in the guided reading approach to small group reading instruction, teachers form small groups that are focused on instruction involving a specific skill or strategy rather than on reading ability alone. This type of flexible within-class grouping allows for differentiation in order to address the needs of each individual student.

  Homogenous grouping by ability is thought to support students in learning at a pace that reflects their skills in the subject. However, research has found that grouping students by reading ability in elementary school is beneficial for high achieving students but has negative consequences for low performing students (Catsambis & Buttaro, 2012; Lleras & Rangel, 2009). In contrast, low ability students may perform best in heterogeneous groups (Lou et al., 1996).

Reading Curriculum in the Primary Grades

Whether formulated at the national, community, or school level, curricular documents define and communicate expectations for students in terms of the knowledge, skills, and attitudes to be developed or acquired through their formal reading instruction. Policies may range from those governing the grade in which formal reading instruction begins to those that prescribe the types of material and the methods to be used in teaching reading.

Curricular aspects and governing policies particularly relevant to the acquisition of reading literacy include standards or benchmarks established for reading development, prevalence of school and classroom libraries, instructional time, methods and materials, and ways of identifying students in need of remediation. Considerable research evidence indicates that students' academic achievement is closely related to the rigor of the curriculum. This involves a coherent progression of instruction and materials through the grade levels, including emphasis on decoding and comprehension strategies, and access to a variety of reading materials. Effective methods for disseminating the curriculum to teachers, parents, and the general public are important, as are ways for making sure that revisions and updates are integrated into instruction.

Especially relevant to ePIRLS is the extent to which a country's curriculum emphasizes online reading, digital reading, and computer skills. Some countries have transformed their standards and curriculum in order to address new media, including teaching elementary school students basic computer skills, such as typing and using a mouse, as well as how to retrieve information via the Internet, and how to use the computer for learning. Other countries place less emphasis on teaching these skills to young students.

Teachers and Teacher Education

Policies on teacher education can facilitate the successful implementation of the intended curriculum, and PIRLS collects information about how countries educate teachers in the content and pedagogical approaches specified in the curriculum. As described in the *PIRLS 2011 Encyclopedia*, such preparation and training may be an integral part of the teacher education curriculum or it may be included in professional development programs for practicing teachers. The requirements to become a primary teacher may include certain types of academic preparation, passing an examination, or meeting other certification criteria. Some countries also have induction or mentoring programs for entering teachers and a number of opportunities for ongoing professional development in order to keep teachers apprised of current developments.

Monitoring Curriculum Implementation

Many countries have systems in place for monitoring and evaluating curriculum implementation, and for assessing student achievement. Commonly used methods include national or regional standardized tests, school inspections, audits, feedback from students and parents, and teaching observations.

Home Contexts

Much research has provided insight into the importance of home environments for reading literacy development. In order to better understand the effects of the home and intergenerational literacy transmission, PIRLS collects data through both the student questionnaire and the Learning to Read Survey, completed by the student's parents or caregivers. Through these two questionnaires, information is gathered on the following:

- Home resources for learning;
- Language(s) spoken in the home;
- Parental educational expectations and academic socialization;
- Early literacy activities and early numeracy activities; and
- Home reading support.

Home Resources for Learning

Home resources for learning encompass important socioeconomic characteristics of the parents, such as their education level, together with home supports for learning and emphasis on educational activities. In educational research, the most influential background factors on student achievement tend to be those that measure socioeconomic status of the parents or caregivers, often indicated through proxy variables such as parental level of education, income, occupational class, and, more generally, home resources such as access to technology, the Internet, and books, including children's books (Bradley & Corwyn, 2002; Dahl & Lochner, 2012; Davis-Kean, 2005; Sirin, 2005; Willms, 2006).

PIRLS has confirmed that there is a sizable association between students' home resources for learning and their reading achievement. For PIRLS 2011, the home resources for learning scale was comprised of the following indicators: parents' education, parents' occupation, the number of books in the home, the number of children's books in the home, and study supports including an Internet connection and the students having a room of their own (Mullis et al., 2012).

Students increasingly have access to new digital media such as *e*books, tablets, and smart phones (Gutnick, Robb, Takeuchi, & Kotler, 2011; Rideout, Foehr, & Roberts, 2010). Research has shown that parents generally are accepting of children spending their time playing on digital media, including certain video games, because they believe that such activities lead to proficiency with computers and technology—important skills for academic and career success (Takeuchi, 2011).

Research still is emerging on the relationship between access to new technology in the home and academic achievement in general, as well as increased reading literacy in particular. Research has shown general computer use to be associated with reading achievement (Lee, Brescia, & Kissinger, 2009). It is believed that, if used correctly, educational applications (apps) for mobile and other new media devices also can be effective, supplementary early learning tools for young children (Chiong & Shuler, 2010; Lieberman, Bates, & So, 2009). As such, there is concern that students with less home access to these costly resources are further disadvantaged in the classroom environment, leading to greater inequity in educational systems (Leu et al., 2009).

Language(s) Spoken in the Home

Because learning to read is dependent on children's early language experiences, the language or languages spoken at home and how they are used are important factors in reading literacy development (Bialystok, 2006; Hoff & Elledge, 2005). If students are not fluent in the language of instruction, often there is at least an initial learning gap because students must learn the concepts and content of the curricula through a new language (Entorf & Minoiu, 2005; Schnepf, 2007; Trong, 2009), with language learners most disadvantaged in subjects with greater language demand, such as reading lessons (Abedi, 2002).

Parental Educational Expectations and Academic Socialization

Parents convey their expectations to their children and provide educational goals for them (Hong & Ho, 2005; Jeynes, 2005). Academic socialization is the process of stressing the importance of education, and includes parents and children talking about the value of education, discussing future educational and occupational expectations for the child, and helping children draw links between schoolwork and its real-world applications (Hill & Tyson, 2009; Taylor, Clayton, & Rowley, 2004).

Academic socialization also can be subject-specific. Research has found that parental socialization in reading is especially important in fostering student achievement in reading (Kloosterman, Notten, Tolsma, & Kraaykamp, 2010). Parents impart their own beliefs about reading that shape children's motivation to read (Baker & Scher, 2002). Socialization can be subtle (e.g., young children seeing adults reading or using texts in different ways learn to appreciate and use printed material) and this process can have long term effects on a student academic performance (Kloosterman et al., 2010).

Early Literacy Activities

In addition to academic socialization, early parental involvement in children's literacy activities can impact early literacy development and can have long-lasting effects on children's literacy as they age (Melhuish et al., 2008; Sénéchal & LeFevre, 2002). Perhaps the most common and important early literacy activity involves adults and older children reading aloud with their young children (Federal Interagency Forum on Child and Family Statistics, 2013; Raikes et al., 2006). By reading with children, children are asked engage with the text and pictures in books; they learn that printed text conveys meaning and that being able to read is valuable and worthwhile, and this experience can increase student motivation to read (Sonnenschein & Munsterman, 2002). In addition, a young child's exposure to oral language is important for literacy acquisition (Hart & Risley, 2003). As children develop their capacity for oral language, they are learning the rules of language use, and this can facilitate the development of literacy skills.

PIRLS has found a positive relationship between early literacy activities in the home and student achievement at the fourth grade. PIRLS routinely asks parents how often they engaged their child in early literacy activities, including reading books, telling stories, singing songs, playing with alphabet toys, talking about things they had done, talking about what they read, playing word games, writing letters or words, and reading aloud signs and labels. For example, the PIRLS Early Literacy Activities Scale, based on these PIRLS 2011 items, was positively related to reading achievement in almost every country (Mullis et al., 2012).

A recent study based on based on TIMSS and PIRLS 2011 data from 34 countries, as measured by the PIRLS Early Literacy Activies Scale (Gustafsson, Hansen, & Rosén, 2013), also showed that engaging children in literacy activities was an important explanatory link in the relationship between parental education and later student achievement at the fourth grade.

Home Reading Support

After children enter formal schooling, reading activities in the home can complement what the child is learning in school (Darling & Westberg, 2004; Kim & Quinn, 2013). Parental intervention in reading has been found to be especially efficacious when educators train parents in specific activities that they can do with their child to promote literacy acquisition (Darling & Westberg, 2004; Sénéchal & Young, 2008; Van Steensel, McElvany, Kurvers, & Herppich, 2011). Parents also can assist their children in their literacy development by listening to their children when they read books aloud (Sénéchal & Young, 2008).

In some countries, it is also common for parents to enroll their children in shadow education programs, private tutoring or classes outside of formal schooling that supplement the academic instruction a child receives at school

(Bray, 1999; Stevenson & Baker, 1992). The purpose for enrolling students in this supplemental schooling varies. Some parents enroll students in programs for remedial work in order for the students to keep pace with their classmates. Other parents hope that additional instruction can make up for any shortcomings in the education provided by the child's school (Baker, Akiba, LeTendre, & Wiseman, 2001). Increasingly, parents enroll students in shadow education programs with the goal of having their children master the curriculum in order to excel on an important examination (Baker & LeTendre, 2005; Buchman, Condron, & Roscigno, 2010), especially where students compete for limited educational opportunities in a tracked program (Baker & LeTendre, 2005).

School Contexts

A school's environment and organization can influence the ease and effectiveness of reaching curricular goals. Accepting that an effective school is not simply a collection of discrete attributes, but rather a well-managed integrated system where each action or policy directly affects all other parts, PIRLS focuses on a set of well-researched school quality indicators:

- School location;
- School composition by student socioeconomic background;
- Instruction affected by resource shortages;
- Teacher working conditions and job satisfaction;
- Principal leadership;
- School emphasis on academic success; and
- Safe, orderly, and disciplined school.

School Location

Depending on the country, schools in urban areas may have access to more resources (e.g., museums, libraries, bookstores) than schools in rural areas. In some countries, schools in urban areas may provide for a more supportive environment because of better staffing conditions and the student population coming from economically more advantaged backgrounds (Erberber, 2009; Johansone, 2009). In contrast, in other countries, schools in urban areas are located in neighborhoods with considerable poverty, little community support, and sometimes even in areas of considerable crime and violence (Milam, Furr-Holden, & Leaf, 2010).

School Composition by Student Socioeconomic Background

Since the Coleman report (Coleman et al., 1966), there has been a great emphasis on how the socioeconomic status of the collective students in the school can influence individual student achievement (Martin, Foy, Mullis, & O'Dwyer, 2013; Rumberger & Palardy, 2005; Sirin, 2005). The correlation between lower socioeconomic status and lower achievement may be able to be partially explained by other school factors. For example, in some countries, schools with students from lower socioeconomic status are taught by less qualified teachers (Akiba, LeTendre, & Scribner, 2007; Clotfelter, Ladd, & Vigdor, 2010). Another theory purports that some schools with many socioeconomically disadvantaged students can be overwhelmed by a culture of futility, in which education and schooling are viewed as an antagonistic exercise having little or no future value (Agirdag, Van Houtte, & Van Avermaet, 2012).

Instruction Affected by Resource Shortages

The extent and quality of school resources also are critical for quality instruction (Greenwald, Hedges, & Laine, 1996; Lee & Barro, 2001; Lee & Zuze, 2011). These may include resources as basic as well-trained teachers or adequate classroom space and other school facilities (Schneider, 2002). Results from PIRLS indicate that students in schools that are well resourced generally have higher achievement than those in schools where shortages of resources affect the capacity to implement the curriculum. Two types of resources—general and subject-specific—affect curriculum implementation. General resources include teaching materials, supplies, school buildings and grounds, heating/cooling and lighting systems, classroom space, audio-visual equipment such as electronic white boards and projectors, and computers, including tablets such as *iPads*. Subject-specific resources for reading include reading materials such as books and *e*books, magazines and periodicals, and digital resources such as educational software/applications (apps) and subscriptions to educational websites. With the importance of online reading for informational purposes, student access to computers, the Internet, and support for their online educational research are increasingly important to expanding literacy competencies.

For reading, a well-resourced school library or multi-media center promotes student reading. The variety and richness of the reading material available to students forms the core of students' reading experience in school. Research has shown that students use the library because there are books that interest them; therefore, ensuring that there are a variety of reading materials that would be of interest to the students at each grade is essential to promoting reading achievement (Clark, 2010). Libraries also are becoming multi-media centers, providing *e*books, access to digital periodicals, and online resources that allow students to seek information on subjects of interest. While school libraries are common in most countries, some countries have moved towards classroom libraries, as is discussed in the Classroom Contexts section of this chapter. Regardless of where the library is located, research has indicated that the availability of books that students can choose from is positively related to reading achievement (Allington et al., 2010).

Teacher Working Conditions and Job Satisfaction

PIRLS 2011 results showed higher achievement for schools that provide good working conditions for teachers. A manageable workload, adequate facilities, and the availability of instructional materials are important ingredients to fostering productive working conditions and promoting teacher satisfaction (Johnson, 2006; Johnson, Kraft, & Papay, 2012).

In addition, a positive school environment can lead to greater job satisfaction and teacher self-efficacy, which in turn can increase student learning (Caprara, Barbaranelli, Steca, & Malone, 2006). Schools can support teachers and increase retention by providing competitive salaries, a reasonable number of teaching hours, adequate workspace, and good equipment. While the physical conditions of the school are important, the social conditions of the school can be essential to retaining teachers and fostering student achievement. Important social factors in a school include a positive school culture, collaboration among teaching staff, and the leadership of the principal (Johnson et al., 2012).

The transition from university to a school teaching position can be difficult. Consequently, in many countries a large percentage of new teachers leave the profession after only a few years of teaching (APPA, 2007; Guarino, Santibañez, & Daley, 2006; Hancock & Scherff, 2010). The extent to which schools take an active role in the acculturation and transition of new teachers may be important for maintaining a stable teaching force. Mentoring programs, modeling of good teacher practice by peers, and induction programs designed by experienced teachers within the school may be important aids to the beginning teacher (Moskowitz & Stephens, 1997; Tillmann, 2005).

Principal Leadership

Research has shown that a principal can affect student achievement. A characteristic of a successful principal is being able to articulate the mission of the school (Witziers, Bosker, & Krüger, 2003). As such, an effective school leader brings coherence to the "complexities of schooling" by aligning the structure and culture of a school with its core purpose (DuFour, Eaker, & DuFour, 2005). This includes guiding the school in setting directions and seeking future opportunities, monitoring that the school's goals are met, as well as building and sustaining an effective learning environment and a positive school climate. Successful principals often are involved in guiding the teaching process as instructional leaders and ensuring that teachers receive the necessary training and development to produce high achievement among the students (Robinson, Lloyd, & Rowe, 2008). Within the constraints of the educational system, it is the principal's responsibility to ensure that the instructional time, and in particular the time devoted to reading, is sufficient for the purposes of curriculum implementation. It is also the principal's responsibility to oversee school-level instructional policies, such as grouping arrangements.

School Emphasis on Academic Success

Overall, the success of a school also can be attributable to a school's emphasis on academic success, or the school's expectation of academic excellence. PIRLS 2011 results, as well as a TIMSS and PIRLS 2011 school effectiveness study (Martin, Foy, Mullis, & O'Dwyer, 2013), have shown an association between academic achievement and the school emphasis on academic success, a construct based on the literature on academic optimism (Hoy, Tarter, & Hoy, 2006; McGuigan & Hoy, 2006; Wu, Hoy, & Tarter, 2013). Indicators of school emphasis on academic success include school administrators' and teachers' expectations for successful curriculum implementation and student achievement, parental support for student achievement, and the students' desire to achieve.

Research also has found that teacher collaboration can increase student learning (Goddard, Goddard, & Tschannen-Moran, 2007; Wheelan & Kesselring, 2005). Teachers who discuss their work with colleagues and collaborate in planning and implementing lessons usually feel less isolated and are less likely to leave teaching (Johnson, Berg, & Donaldson, 2005). The collective education of a school's teachers also can be essential to its academic success. From as early as first grade, research has linked the collective teacher education in a school to student achievement (Croninger, Rice, Rathbun, & Nishio, 2007), suggesting that collaboration among teachers with strong educational backgrounds can create an emphasis on academic success within the school and facilitate the implementation of the curriculum.

Collective efficacy among the teachers of the school and general trust that faculty members have for parents and students are additional attributes of a well-functioning school (Hoy et al., 2006; McGuigan & Hoy, 2006; Wu et al., 2013). Schools that encourage and welcome parental involvement are more likely to have highly involved parents than schools that do not make an effort to keep parents informed and participating (Jeynes, 2005). High levels of parental involvement can improve student achievement, as well as students' overall attitude toward school (Dearing, Kreider, & Weiss, 2008; Jeynes, 2005; Jeynes, 2007; Taylor, Pearson, Clark, & Walpole, 2000).

In effective schools, the principal and teachers collaborate to ensure that the curriculum is appropriately implemented in the classrooms. In addition to testing and value-added models, research has found that classroom observations and student surveys can provide important information about the effectiveness of teaching practices (Bill & Melinda Gates Foundation, 2013).

Safe, Orderly, and Disciplined School

Respect for individual students and teachers, a safe and orderly environment, and constructive interactions among administrators, teachers, parents, and students all contribute to a positive school climate and lead to higher student achievement (Cohen, McCabe, Michelli, & Pickeral, 2009; Greenberg, Skidmore, & Rhodes, 2004; Konishi, Hymel, Zumbo, & Li, 2010; Martin, Foy, Mullis, & O'Dwyer, 2013). The sense of security that comes from having few behavioral problems and little or no concern about student or teacher safety at school promotes a stable learning environment. A general lack of discipline, especially if students and teachers are afraid for their safety, does not facilitate learning and is associated with lower academic achievement (Milam et al., 2010; Stanco, 2012). Schools where there are clear rules and more fairness have atmospheres of greater discipline and safety (Gottfredson, Gottfredson, Payne, & Gottfredson, 2005).

Bullying among students is a threat to the school learning environment. Bullying is aggressive behavior that is intended to harm students who are physically or psychologically less strong and takes a variety of forms ranging from name calling to inflicting physical harm. Bullying causes distress to victims, leads to low self-esteem, and makes victims feel like they do not belong (Glew, Fan, Katon, & Rivara, 2008), and research shows that bullied students are less likely to achieve in school (Glew et al., 2008; Konishi et al., 2010; Rothon, Head, Klineberg, & Stansfeld, 2011). With the prevalence of the Internet, cyberbullying is a new form of bullying that unfortunately appears to be common among students; and, like other bullying, cyberbullying leads to low self-esteem, distress, and poor achievement (Mishna, Cook, Gadalla, Daciuk, & Solomon, 2010; Tokunaga, 2010). Unlike bullying, the process of cyberbullying can be shrouded in a cloud of anonymity for the Internet bully.

Classroom Contexts

Because most of the teaching and learning in school takes place in the classroom, successful learning is influenced by the classroom environment and instructional activities. PIRLS 2016 focuses on the following proven practices that improve teaching and learning:

- Teacher preparation and experience;
- Classroom resources;
- Instructional time;
- Instructional engagement;
- Instruction for online reading; and
- Classroom assessment.

This section benefitted especially from John Hattie's (2009) book, *Visible Learning: A Synthesis of Over 800 Meta-analyses Relating to Achievement*.

Teacher Preparation and Experience

The preparation and competence of teachers is critical (Darling-Hammond, 2000; Hill, Rowan, & Ball, 2005), and prospective teachers need coursework in order to gain knowledge in the subjects that they will teach, to understand about how students learn, and to learn about effective pedagogy in teaching reading.

In addition to teacher education and training, teacher experience is essential, and the first years of teaching experience are especially important for teacher development (Harris & Sass, 2011; Leigh, 2010). However, research also has found that teachers continue to develop after five years of experience, and that this development can positively affect student achievement (Harris et al., 2011).

Professional development through seminars, workshops, conferences, and professional journals can help teachers increase their effectiveness and broaden their knowledge (Blank & de las Alas, 2009; Yoon, Duncan, Lee, Scarloss, & Shapley, 2007). Professional development is especially important in order to train teachers in how to incorporate online reading into their classroom practices (Coiro, 2012).

With education, training, and experience, teachers should feel prepared and confident to teach reading literacy. Research has shown that teachers' confidence in their teaching skills not only is associated with their professional behavior, but also with students' performance and motivation (Bandura, 1997; Henson, 2002).

Classroom Resources

Another aspect of the classroom that is relevant for reading literacy includes the extent of the variety and richness of the reading material available to students. The reading material and technology that teachers use in reading instruction form the core of students' reading experience in school.

Students who have easy access to reading materials are more likely to read. For this reason, many countries have moved to creating classroom libraries that provide a wide variety of text and text types, including digital resources, as well as a special place for independent reading. It is believed that the presence of a classroom library can aid teachers in incorporating literature into instruction and foster positive reading habits and attitudes (Morrow, 2003; Routman, 2003; Young & Moss, 2006).

In the digital age, a growing aspect of reading instruction is how to incorporate new media into reading instruction; therefore, the use of technology in the classroom, and teachers' familiarity and comfort with technology, is increasingly important. Teachers' decisions to use technology in the classroom can result from their beliefs, attitudes, and comfort levels, as well as access to training and materials (Mueller, Wood, Willoughby, Ross, & Specht, 2008; Russell, Bebell, O'Dwyer, & O'Connor, 2003). Access to technology also is an important factor (Hsu, Wang, & Runco, 2013).

Instructional Time

At the school level, the relative emphasis and amount of time specified for reading instruction can greatly affect the opportunities to learn. Results from PIRLS show that there is variation between countries in the intended instructional time prescribed by the curriculum and the actual time of implementation in the classroom. On average, however, there is very close agreement between the curriculum guidelines and teachers' reports about implementation. Research has shown that it is especially important that instructional time be used effectively toward the learning goals, and not be spent on secondary activities unrelated to the instructional content.

Homework is one way teachers can extend instruction and evaluate student learning. The types of homework assigned in reading classes regularly include independent reading, comprehension questions about what students have read, or some combination of the two. The amount of homework assigned for reading varies both within and across countries. In some countries, homework typically is assigned to students who need it the most. In other countries, students receive homework as an enrichment exercise. Strong students may spend less time on homework because they use their time more efficiently (Trautwein, 2007; Won & Han, 2010). For these reasons, it has been argued that the effect of homework may be better encapsulated by measures of homework frequency than homework time (Trautwein, 2007). In addition, there is evidence that homework is more effective for older students and higher achieving students (Hattie, 2009).

Instructional Engagement

TIMSS and PIRLS 2011 school effectiveness research has confirmed the importance of student engagement with instruction as an important factor in predicting reading achievement (Martin, Foy, Mullis, & O'Dwyer, 2013). According to McLaughlin et al. (2005), student engagement focuses the student's "in-the-moment" cognitive interaction with the content. "Learning occurs through the cognitive engagement of the learner with the appropriate subject matter knowledge" (McLaughlin et al., 2005, p.5). Engagement can take place when a student listens to the teacher, discusses texts with peers, or reads independently. Engagement has been conceptualized as the idea that a student's "in-the-moment" mindset is torn between engagement with instruction and distractions that are unrelated to the topics in the class (Yair, 2000). The challenge for the teacher is to use effective methods of instruction in order to maintain student engagement in the content, activating the students cognitively (Klieme, Pauli, & Reusser, 2009; Lipowsky et al., 2009). A well-managed classroom and a supportive classroom environment can facilitate this engagement process (Klieme et al., 2009; Lipowsky et al., 2009).

Effective classroom management allows for better engagement with teaching and learning, as well as higher achievement outcomes, because it focuses the class and instructional time on the topic (Fauth, Decristan, Rieser, Kleime, & Büttner, 2014; Lipowsky et al., 2009; Marzano, Marzano, & Pickering, 2003; Wang, Haertel, & Walberg, 1993). Effective teachers are strong classroom managers, who build trust with the students and limit disruptions to the instruction (Stronge, Ward, & Grant, 2011). Teachers can be strong classroom managers by ensuring that rules are clear, taking effective disciplinary action, building optimal student-teacher relationships, and maintaining an alert and objective mindset during instruction (Marzano et al., 2003).

Fostering student motivation in reading is fundamental for reading teachers, because students who are motivated to read more, especially at a young age, become better readers (Lewis & Samuels, 2003). Motivation can be facilitated, according to self-determination theory (Deci & Ryan, 1985), by creating a supportive environment that fosters a sense of *relatedness*, *competence*, and *autonomy*. A classroom environment that is overly controlling can stifle student motivation because it removes the student's sense of autonomy (Niemiec & Ryan, 2009). Effective teachers are able to create an optimal classroom environment by providing clear purpose and "strong guidance" for the classroom while encouraging cooperation among the students and an environment of respect between students as well as between students and the teacher (Marzano et al., 2003). Supportive teacher-student relationships are important not only in order to foster student motivation (Cornelius-White, 2007; Marzano et al., 2003), but also to increase student participation and student achievement (Cornelius-White, 2007; Fauth et al., 2014). A socially welcoming school environment or classroom also can provide a sense of relatedness by giving students a sense of belonging (Goodenow & Grady, 1993).

Additionally, teachers can nurture student motivation in reading by creating an environment that allows students to work autonomously, while providing support and guidance (Ryan & Deci, 2000; Reeve, Jang, Carrell, Jeon, & Barch, 2004). Autonomy can be fostered in reading instruction by allowing students the opportunity to choose their reading material (Guthrie, McRae, & Klauda, 2007).

An effective teacher ensures that students are actively involved in their own learning process. Students are more engaged in student-centered learning when they are working individually or with their peers rather than listening to a teacher lecture or watching a video (Shernoff, Csikszentmihalyi, Schneider, &

Shernoff, 2003; Yair, 2000). Peer-tutoring, small group work, and peer mentoring are effective strategies that promote student engagement and are linked to achievement (Hattie, 2009; Springer, Stanne, & Donovan, 1999).

Students also are more engaged when they are challenged and face greater cognitive demands (Shernoff et al., 2003; Yair, 2000). However, the challenges of the tasks should be perceived to be attainable for the students. In this respect, effective teaching is setting challenging yet attainable goals for each student and supporting the students in reaching the goals (Hattie, 2009; Klein, Wesson, Hollenbeck, & Alge, 1999). In setting goals, it is important that students understand the process of achievement, what outcome is expected, and why the goal is important for the learning process (Hattie, 2009; Martin, 2006). One way that students can be supported in reaching their goals is by linking the new material and concepts to the students' prior knowledge and understanding (Klieme et al., 2009; McLaughlin et al., 2005). Concept mapping (Nesbit & Adesope, 2006) and advance organizers (Hattie, 2009; Stone, 1983) are two proven strategies for linking prior learned concepts to new concepts.

Discussion-based instructional approaches have been shown to be effective in engaging and supporting students in their reading development (Applebee, Langer, Nystrand, & Gamoran, 2003; Murphy, Wilkinson, Soter, Hennessey, & Alexander, 2009). The specific discussion-based strategy implemented by the teacher (e.g. collaborative reading, questioning the author) can have a distinct effect on the development of a child's reading comprehension and critical thinking skills, and therefore the approach should be aligned with the goals of the lesson (Murphy et al., 2009).

Effective teachers also find means to emphasize the relevance of the learning task (Yair, 2000). By providing stimulating reading tasks around student interest and students' hands-on experiences, teachers can fuel student interest in reading, increasing motivation and reading comprehension (Guthrie et al., 2006).

Overall, research has shown that there are many strategies to teach reading and enhance comprehension. It is the educator's responsiblity to understand the needs of the students and to incorporate the instructional techniques that can best foster student motivation to read and student achievement. Effective reading instruction provides a balanced program, integrating many components, including multiple texts, teacher- and student-led discussions, collaborative learning, time for independent reading, and a variety of assessment techniques (Gambrell, Malloy, & Mazzoni, 2011). Other proven instructional strategies include repeated reading (Therrien, 2004), phonemic awareness instruction (Ehri et al., 2001), and vocabulary instruction (Elleman, Lindo, Morphy, & Compton, 2009).

Instruction for Online Reading

An emerging aspect of reading instruction is the teaching of online reading. Unlike traditional reading, students reading online must learn to negotiate their way through Internet features such as hypertexts, multi-modal texts, and interactive texts, in order to find the information they are seeking (Coiro, 2003). Informational searches begin with a question, and with this question in mind the student uses a search engine in order to locate the information, as well as to identify and evaluate the credibility of the search results and the sites visited (Leu et al., 2007). In addition, online readers often need to synthesize the information from multiple websites in order to answer the question (Leu et al., 2007). While traditional print-based offline reading informs online reading comprehension, the skills needed for successful online reading go beyond those needed for print reading (Coiro, 2011; Leu et al., 2007). From an instructor's point of view, for students to become strong online readers, they not only must know how to read, but they also must be able to locate, evaluate, and synthesize information in the online environment (Coiro, 2011; Leu et al., 2007), a process that assumes basic computer skills and the ability to use technology as a tool to find information (Tondeur, van Braak, & Valcke, 2007). Therefore, it is increasingly important for teachers to tailor lessons to this new form of reading (Leu et al., 2007).

In some circumstances, poor offline readers may be more skilled or engaged in the interactive nature of seeking information through online media, and therefore can compensate for weaknesses in reading with their online skills (Castek, Zawilinski, McVerry, O'Byrne, & Leu, 2010; Leu et al., 2007). For example, students using digital technology are more likely to use resources that aid comprehension, such as dictionaries (Wright, Fugett, & Caputa, 2013). It also has been shown that students with less prior knowledge in a topic are able to perform well on Internet-related tasks, because their Internet skills can help overcome knowledge deficits (Coiro, 2011).

Classroom Assessment

Teachers have a number of ways to monitor student progress and achievement. PIRLS results show that teachers devote a fair amount of time to student assessment, whether as a means of gauging what students have learned or for providing feedback to students, teachers, and parents. The frequency and format of assessment are important indicators of teaching and school pedagogy, and research has shown that frequent testing can lead to improving student achievement (Başol & Johanson, 2009). Informal assessments during instruction help teachers identify needs of particular individuals, evaluate the pace of the presentation, and adapt the instruction. Formal tests, both teacher-made and standardized assessments, typically are used to make important decisions about students (e.g., grades) or schools for accountability purposes. Teachers use a variety of formats and test a wide range of contents and cognitive skills. The types of questions included in tests and quizzes can send strong signals to students about what is important.

Student Characteristics and Attitudes Toward Learning

An important topic in educational research is the relationship between student attitudes toward a subject and students' academic achievement. In educational research, there are numerous theories regarding how student motivation and confidence can lead to engagement and academic achievement. PIRLS 2016 includes information about the following:

- Student readiness to learn;
- Student motivation;
- Student self-concept; and
- Student reading literacy behaviors.

Student Readiness to Learn

In order for students to engage in a task or a goal, it is crucial that they are physiologically ready and possess the prerequisite knowledge to engage in the content (McLaughlin et al., 2005). Results from PIRLS 2011 indicated that many students, even in the most developed countries, struggle to pay attention in class due to hunger and sleep deprivation.

Research has identified nutritional problems to be a barrier to student learning, with school breakfast programs suggested as a possible solution (Taras, 2005). Likewise, sleep deprivation has been found to be related to lower achievement (Dewald, Meijer, Oort, Kerkhof, & Bögels, 2010), and may be associated with the early start times at certain schools (Perkinson-Gloor, Lemola, & Grob, 2013), as well as the socioeconomic status of the student (Buckhalt, 2011).

In addition to physiological readiness, students also need to have the prerequisite knowledge to engage with the content because "every new thing that a person learns must be attached to what the person already knows" (McLaughlin et al., 2005, p. 5). In other words, for students to learn, they need to be able to connect the new content to prior knowledge.

Student Motivation

In addition to students' readiness to learn, their motivation is essential to success in reading (Anmarkrud & Bråten, 2009; Logan, Medford, & Hughes, 2011). The source of academic motivation and how it can be facilitated within the school, classroom, and home has been a recurrent area of research (Bandura, 1997; Csikszentmihalyi, 1990; Deci & Ryan, 1985). Students have different levels of motivation for each distinct task and subject area.

Most of the literature separates motivation into two distinct constructs: intrinsic motivation and extrinsic motivation. Intrinsic motivation is an "energizer of behavior" (Deci & Ryan, 1985, p.32). Students who are intrinsically motivated to read find it to be interesting and enjoyable (Deci & Ryan, 1985) and have a positive attitude towards reading. Although it is theorized that all human beings are born with intrinsic motivation to learn, contexts such as the home and school can either facilitate or suppress this inner motivation.

Extrinsic motivation refers to the drive that comes from external rewards like praise, career success, money, and other incentives. Research consistently shows that intrinsic motivation is more closely related to reading achievement than extrinsic motivation (Becker, McElvany, & Kortenbruck, 2010; Schiefele, Schaffner, Möller, & Wigfield, 2012; Vansteenkiste, Timmermans, Lens, Soenens, & Van den Broeck, 2008). Indeed, some research points to external rewards dampening a student's intrinsic motivation (Deci, Koestner, & Ryan, 1999). Nevertheless, most students do not have an intrinsic motivation to learn all subjects, and therefore fostering motivation through extrinsic rewards may be a necessary course of action for a teacher or a parent. In these cases, research has found that successful students internalize their extrinsic motivation to increase performance, in an environment that cultivates feelings of relatedness, competence, and autonomy (Ryan & Deci, 2000; Deci & Moller, 2005).

Student Self-concept

Students' perceived competence in a subject is linked to their subject-specific self-concept. If students believe that reading tasks are outside the scope of what can be completed successfully, students will view the exercise as futile, and this will affect their motivation. In contrast, if students are confident, they are more likely to persevere in order to successfully complete the school task (Bandura, 1997). Self-concept often is estimated relative to students' peers or experiences, and is a multi-dimensional construct (Marsh & Craven, 2006); that is, students reading self-concept is distinct from their mathematics or science self-concept.

Student Reading Literacy Behaviors

Students who are motivated to read and have a strong reading self-concept tend to read more than their peers and have better reading comprehension (De Naeghel, Van Keer, Vansteenkiste, & Rosseel, 2012). The process can be cyclical, because students who are good readers, with strong reading skills, tend to read recreationally (Leppänen, Aunola, & Nurmi, 2005; Mol & Bus, 2011), which contributes to consolidating their reading ability by improving vocabularies, spelling abilities, and so forth (Mol & Bus, 2011).

Recreational reading habits often are supported by the family and friends of young readers; thus, a supportive home environment can be influential in fostering children's reading habits. However, home support is not only important for children prior to their entry into primary school; home support also can be influential in promoting reading throughout children's schooling (Baker, 2003; Klauda & Wigfield, 2012).

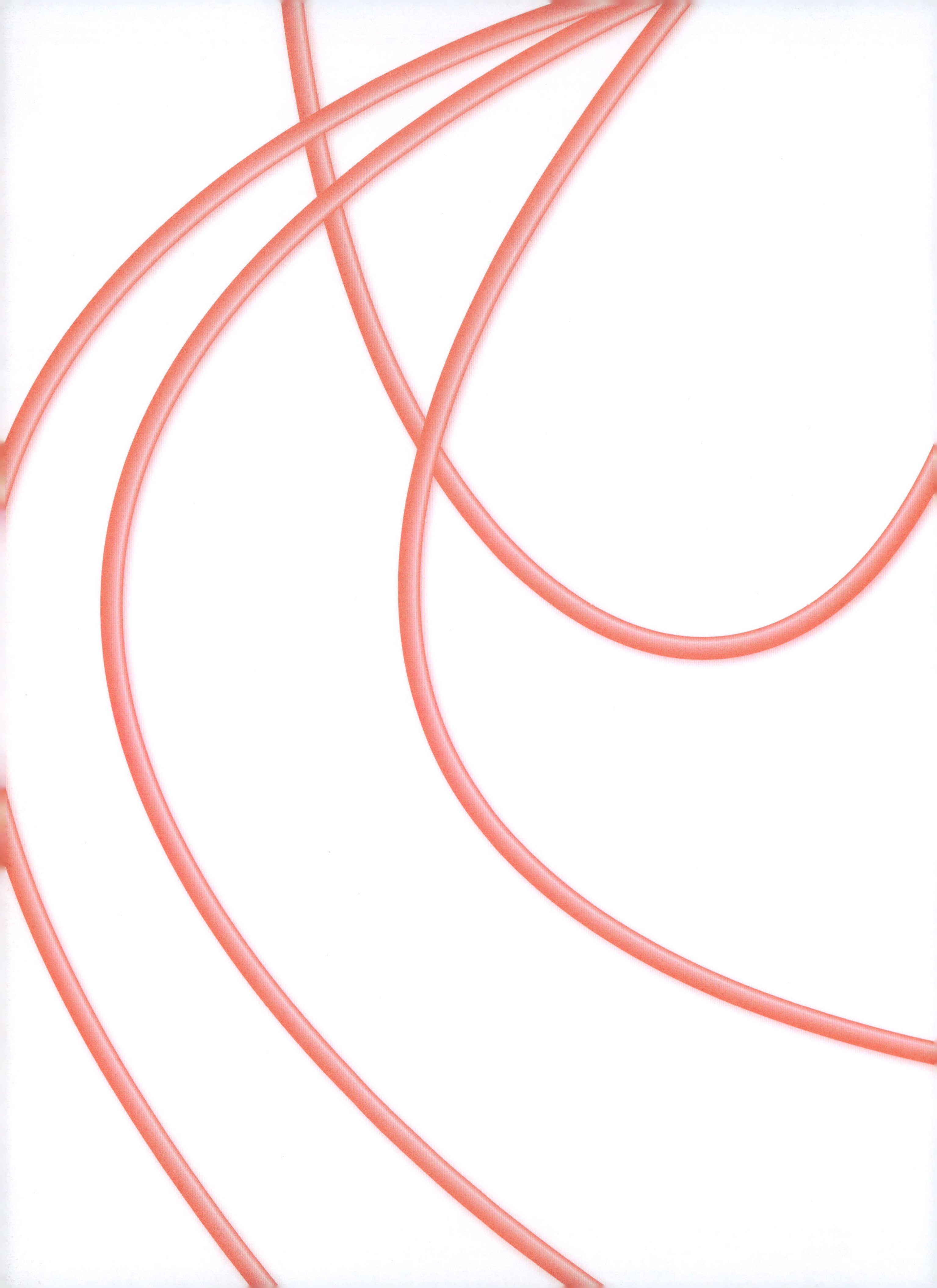

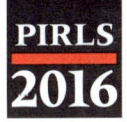

CHAPTER 3

Assessment Design for PIRLS, PIRLS Literacy, and ePIRLS in 2016

Michael O. Martin, Ina V.S. Mullis, and Pierre Foy

PIRLS 2016 consists of three separate assessments of reading comprehension: PIRLS, PIRLS Literacy, and ePIRLS. PIRLS is a comprehensive assessment of fourth grade students' reading literacy achievement. Conducted on a regular five-year cycle, with each assessment linked to those that preceded it, PIRLS provides regular data on trends in students' reading literacy on a common achievement scale. Matching PIRLS for breadth of coverage but with less difficult reading passages and items, PIRLS Literacy extends the effective measurement of reading comprehension at the lower end of the PIRLS achievement scale. For countries participating in PIRLS, ePIRLS expands PIRLS to include the assessment of online reading to acquire and use information. The PIRLS assessments include a series of contextual questionnaires to gather information about community, home, and school contexts for developing reading literacy.

Student Population Assessed

PIRLS assesses the reading literacy of children in their fourth year of formal schooling. This population was chosen for PIRLS because it is an important transition point in children's development as readers. Typically, at this point, students have learned how to read and are now reading to learn. In many countries, this also is when students begin to have separate classes for different subjects, such as mathematics and science. The target population for PIRLS is defined as follows:

> The PIRLS target grade should be the grade that represents four years of schooling, counting from the first year of ISCED Level 1.

ISCED is the International Standard Classification of Education developed by the UNESCO Institute for Statistics and provides an international standard for describing levels of schooling across countries (UNESCO, 2012). The ISCED system describes the full range of schooling, from early childhood education (Level 0) to doctoral study (Level 8). ISCED Level 1 corresponds to primary education, or the first stage of basic education. The PIRLS target grade is four years after the beginning of Level 1, which is the fourth grade in most countries. However, given the linguistic and cognitive demands of reading, PIRLS wants to avoid assessing very young children. Thus, if the average age of fourth grade students at the time of testing would be less than 9.5 years, PIRLS recommends that countries assess the next higher grade (i.e., fifth grade).

Reporting Reading Achievement

PIRLS and PIRLS Literacy are designed to provide a complete picture of the reading literacy achievement of the participating students in each country. This includes achievement by reading purpose and comprehension process as well as overall reading achievement. Consistent with the goal of a comprehensive view of reading comprehension, the entire PIRLS assessment consists of 12 reading passages and accompanying questions (known as items); similarly, the PIRLS Literacy assessment consists of 12 reading passages and accompanying questions, but the passages are less difficult. In each assessment, six passages assess reading for literary experience and six assess reading to acquire and use information. In order to keep the assessment burden on any one student to a minimum, each student is presented with just two passages according to a systematic booklet assembly and rotation procedure, as described in the next section. Following data collection, student responses for both the PIRLS and PIRLS Literacy assessments are placed on the PIRLS reading achievement scale using item response theory methods that provide an overall picture of the assessment results for each country.[1]

Integration between PIRLS and PIRLS Literacy is maintained by including two PIRLS Literacy passages in the PIRLS assessment and two PIRLS passages in the PIRLS Literacy assessment. This provides a solid foundation for employing the PIRLS scaling and linking methodology to ensure that students taking the PIRLS Literacy assessment have their achievement reported on the PIRLS scale. Moreover, including the two less difficult PIRLS Literacy passages benefits PIRLS by providing more information about the reading accomplishments of students who participate in the PIRLS assessment and perform at the lower end of the

---

[1] The PIRLS scaling methodology is described in detail in Foy, Brossman & Galia (2012).

achievement scale. Conversely, including the more difficult PIRLS passages in the PIRLS Literacy assessment provides information about the accomplishments of higher performing students who participate in PIRLS Literacy.

The PIRLS assessments are designed from the outset to measure trends over time in reading achievement. Accordingly, the PIRLS reading achievement scale provides a common metric on which countries can compare their fourth grade students' progress in reading over time from assessment to assessment. The PIRLS achievement scale was established in 2001 so that 100 points on the scale corresponded to one standard deviation across all of the countries that participated in 2001, and the scale centerpoint of 500 corresponded to the international average across those countries. Using passages that were administered in both the 2001 and 2006 assessments as a basis for linking the two sets of assessment results, the PIRLS 2006 data also were placed on this scale so that countries could gauge changes in students' reading achievement since 2001. Following a similar procedure, the PIRLS 2011 data also were placed on the PIRLS scale, as will be the data from PIRLS 2016. This will enable countries that have participated in PIRLS since its inception to have comparable achievement data from 2001, 2006, 2011, and 2016, and to plot changes in performance over this 15-year period.

The PIRLS reading achievement scale is an overall measure of reading proficiency that includes both reading purposes and processes of comprehension. However, in addition to the overall scale, PIRLS and PIRLS Literacy also provide separate achievement scales on the same metric for purposes for reading and for processes of comprehension. More specifically, there are two scales for reading purposes:

- Reading for literary experience; and
- Reading to acquire and use information.

In addition to these, there also are two scales for processes of reading comprehension:

- Retrieval and straightforward inferencing; and
- Interpreting, integrating, and evaluating.[2]

Countries participating in ePIRLS also participate in PIRLS; so, in addition to the usual PIRLS overall reading achievement results and results by reading purpose and comprehension process, ePIRLS participants can report student

---

[2] Retrieval and straightforward inferencing combines items from the Focus on and Retrieve Explicitly Stated Information and Make Straightforward Inferences comprehension processes. Similarly, interpreting, integrating, and evaluating is based on items from the Interpret and Integrate Ideas and Information and Examine and Critique Content and Textual Elements processes.

achievement in online reading for informational purposes. The ePIRLS online reading achievement scale enables countries to examine their students' online reading performance relative to their performance on the PIRLS reading achievement scales.

PIRLS and PIRLS Literacy Booklet Design

Given the broad coverage and reporting goals of the PIRLS framework and its emphasis on the use of a variety of authentic texts, the specifications for the pool of assessment items include extensive testing time. The PIRLS Reading Development Group found that a valid assessment of two purposes for reading—reading for literary experience and reading to acquire and use information—with reliable measures of two processes of comprehension required good coverage of the range of reading material that children encounter in school and their everyday lives.

With a total testing time for the assessment passages of eight hours, but far less time available to assess any individual student, the PIRLS assessment materials must be divided in some way. Therefore, because of the difficulties of scheduling student assessments and because young children cannot be subjected to long testing periods without suffering loss of concentration and fatigue, the testing time is limited to 80 minutes per student, with an additional 15–30 minutes for a student questionnaire.

To address this challenge, the PIRLS assessment design uses a matrix sampling technique: each reading passage and its accompanying items is assigned to a block, and the blocks are then systematically distributed among individual student booklets. Both PIRLS and PIRLS Literacy consist of 12 passages/blocks, each of which is expected to require 40 minutes of student testing time.

As shown in Exhibit 3, the five literary blocks developed specifically for PIRLS are labeled PRLit1 through PRLit5 and the five informational blocks PRInf1 through PRInf5. The two blocks from PIRLS Literacy are labeled PLLit3 and PLInf3. Six of the ten PIRLS blocks were included in previous PIRLS assessments: two in all three assessments (2001, 2006, and 2011), two in both PIRLS 2006 and PIRLS 2011, and two in PIRLS 2011 only. These "trend" blocks provide a foundation for measuring trends in reading achievement. In addition, the 2016 assessment includes four new PIRLS blocks developed for use for the first time.

Exhibit 3: PIRLS 2016 Matrix Sampling Blocks

Purpose for Reading	Block					
Literary Experience	PRLit1	PRLit2	PRLit3	PRLit4	PRLit5	PLLit3
Acquire and Use Information	PRInf1	PRInf2	PRInf3	PRInf4	PRInf5	PLInf3

The ten blocks developed specifically for PIRLS Literacy are shown in Exhibit 4, with the five blocks of literary passages labeled PLLit1 through PLLit5 and the five informational blocks PLInf1 through PLInf5. The two blocks from PIRLS are labeled PRLit1 and PRInf1. Four of the passage and item blocks were previously used in 2011 as part of prePIRLS. Because prePIRLS has been subsumed into PIRLS Literacy for the 2016 assessment cycle, these passages from 2011 provide the basis for measuring trends in 2016. The remaining six PIRLS Literacy blocks are newly developed for 2016.

Exhibit 4: PIRLS Literacy 2016 Matrix Sampling Blocks

Purpose for Reading	Block					
Literary Experience	PLLit1	PLLit2	PLLit3	PLLit4	PLLit5	PRLit1
Acquire and Use Information	PLInf1	PLInf2	PLInf3	PLInf4	PLInf5	PRInf1

The PIRLS 2016 booklet design shows how the blocks of passages and items are assembled into individual student booklets, each consisting of two 40-minute blocks of passages and items. Individual students respond to one assessment booklet and a student questionnaire.

The PIRLS booklet design (see Exhibit 5) includes the ten blocks of PIRLS passages and items described in Exhibit 3, as well as two of the PIRLS Literacy blocks from Exhibit 4 (PLLit3 and PLInf3). These 12 blocks are distributed across 16 booklets. Booklets 1–15 each consist of one literary passage and items and one informational passage and items. In order to present at least some passages in a more natural, authentic setting, one literary block (PRLit5) and one informational block (PRInf5) are presented in a magazine-type format with the questions in a separate booklet. This 16th booklet is referred to as the PIRLS "Reader."

Exhibit 5: PIRLS 2016 Student Booklet Design

Booklet	Part 1	Part 2
1	PRInf2	PRLit1
2	PRLit3	PRInf2
3	PLInf3	PRLit3
4	PLInf3	PRLit4
5	PRLit4	PRInf1
6	PRLit2	PRInf1
7	PRInf3	PRLit2
8	PLLit3	PRInf3
9	PLLit3	PRInf4
10	PRInf4	PRLit1
11	PRLit3	PRInf1
12	PLInf3	PRLit2
13	PRInf3	PRLit1
14	PLLit3	PRInf2
15	PRInf4	PRLit4
Reader	PRLit5	PRInf5

The 16 PIRLS booklets are distributed among students in participating classrooms so that the groups of students completing each booklet are approximately equivalent in terms of student reading ability. PIRLS uses item response theory scaling methods to assemble a comprehensive picture of the reading achievement of a country's entire fourth grade student population by pooling individual students' responses to the booklets that they are assigned. This approach reduces to manageable proportions what otherwise would be an impossible student burden, albeit at the cost of greater complexity in booklet assembly, data collection, and data analysis.

In order to enable linking among booklets within PIRLS, and to maintain links between PIRLS and PIRLS Literacy, it is desirable that the student booklets contain as many block pair combinations as possible. However, because the number of booklets can become very large if each block is to be paired with all other blocks, it is necessary to choose judiciously among possible block combinations.

In the PIRLS 16-booklet design, each of five literary blocks (PRLit1–PRLit4 and PLLit3) and each of five informational blocks (PRInf1–PRInf4 and PLInf3) appear in three of the PIRLS booklets, each time paired with another, different block. For example, as shown in Exhibit 5, literary block PRLit1 appears with informational block PRInf2 in Booklet 1 and with informational blocks PRInf4 and PRInf3 in Booklets 10 and 13, respectively. Informational block PRInf2 appears not only with PRLit1 in Booklet 1, but also with literary block PRLit3 in Booklet 2 and with PIRLS Literacy literary block PLLit3 in Booklet 14. Each of the two PIRLS Literacy blocks (PLLit3 and PLInf3) appears in three PIRLS booklets. By design, the two PIRLS Literacy block passages are less demanding than the PIRLS passages. Accordingly, when a PIRLS Literacy block is paired with a PIRLS block the Literacy block always is in first position in the booklet. Including the two PIRLS Literacy blocks in the PIRLS booklet scheme ensures a link between PIRLS and PIRLS Literacy. This link is further strengthened by including two PIRLS blocks in the PIRLS Literacy booklet scheme (see below).

The blocks in the PIRLS Reader, PRLit5 and PRInf5, are not linked to any other blocks directly. However, because booklets are assigned to students using a randomized procedure, the group of students responding to the Reader is equivalent to those responding to the other booklets, within the margin of error of the sampling process. Because each block appears in three of Booklets 1 through 15, the Reader is assigned three times more frequently in the distribution procedure than these booklets, so that the same proportion of students respond to blocks PRLit5 and PRInf5 as to each of the other blocks in the PIRLS booklets.

Similar to the PIRLS booklet design, the PIRLS Literacy booklet design consists of Booklets 1–15 and a PIRLS Literacy Reader, with each booklet consisting of two 40-minute blocks of passages and items, and each student responding to one assessment booklet and a student questionnaire (see Exhibit 6). Each booklet contains one literary passage and one informational passage. The PIRLS Literacy design includes the ten blocks of PIRLS Literacy passages and items shown in Exhibit 4 (PLLit1–PLLit5 and PLInf1–PLInf5) together with two of the PIRLS blocks from Exhibit 3 (PRLit1 and PRInf1). The PIRLS Literacy Reader consists of literary block PLLit5 and informational block PLInf5.

Exhibit 6: PIRLS Literacy 2016 Student Booklet Design

Booklet	Part 1	Part 2
1	PLInf1	PRLit1
2	PLLit2	PLInf1
3	PLInf3	PLLit2
4	PLInf3	PLLit4
5	PLLit4	PRInf1
6	PLLit1	PRInf1
7	PLInf2	PLLit1
8	PLLit3	PLInf2
9	PLLit3	PLInf4
10	PLInf4	PRLit1
11	PLLit2	PRInf1
12	PLInf3	PLLit1
13	PLInf2	PRLit1
14	PLLit3	PLInf1
15	PLInf4	PLLit4
Reader	PLLit5	PLInf5

Also paralleling the PIRLS design, each of five literary blocks (PLLit1–PLLit4 and PRLit1) and five informational blocks (PLInf1–PLInf4 and PRInf1) appears in three of the 15 PIRLS Literacy booklets, each time paired with another, different, block. Each of the two PIRLS blocks (PRLit1 and PRInf1) appears in three PIRLS Literacy booklets. Because these PIRLS blocks are more difficult than the PIRLS Literacy blocks, they appear in the second position in the booklet when paired with a Literacy block.

Question Types and Scoring Procedures

Students' ability to comprehend text through the four PIRLS comprehension processes is assessed via comprehension questions that accompany each text. Two question formats are used in the PIRLS and PIRLS Literacy assessments: multiple-choice and constructed-response. Each multiple-choice question is worth one point. Constructed-response questions are worth one, two, or three points, depending on the depth of understanding required. Up to half of the total number of points represented by all of the questions come from multiple-choice questions. In the development of comprehension questions, the decision to use either a multiple-choice or a constructed-response format is based on the process being assessed, and on which format best enables test takers to demonstrate their reading comprehension.

Multiple-choice Questions

Multiple-choice questions provide students with four response options, of which only one is correct. Multiple-choice questions can be used to assess any of the comprehension processes. However, because they do not allow for students' explanations or supporting statements, multiple-choice questions may be less suitable for assessing students' ability to make more complex interpretations or evaluations.

In assessing fourth grade students, it is important that linguistic features of the questions be developmentally appropriate. Therefore, questions are written clearly and concisely. Response options also are written succinctly in order to minimize the reading demand of the question. Incorrect options are written to be plausible, but not deceptive. For students who may be unfamiliar with this test question format, the instructions given at the beginning of the test include a sample multiple-choice item that illustrates how to select and mark an answer.

Constructed-response Questions

Constructed-response test items require students to provide a written response, rather than select a response from a set of options. The emphasis placed on constructed-response questions in the PIRLS assessments is consistent with the definition of literacy underlying the framework. It reflects the interactive, constructive view of reading—meaning is constructed through an interaction between the reader, the text, and the context of the reading task. This question type may be used to assess any of the four comprehension processes. However, it is particularly well suited for assessing aspects of comprehension that require students to provide support or that result in interpretations involving students' background knowledge and experiences.

In the PIRLS assessments, constructed-response questions may be worth one or two points (short-answer items), or three points (extended-response items), depending on the depth of understanding or the extent of textual support the question requires. In framing these questions, it is important to provide enough information to help students clearly understand the nature of the response expected.

Each constructed-response question has an accompanying scoring guide that describes the essential features of appropriate and complete responses. Scoring guides focus on evidence of the type of comprehension the questions assess. The guides describe evidence of partial understanding and evidence of complete or extensive understanding. In addition, sample student responses at each level of understanding provide important guidance to scoring staff.

In scoring students' responses to constructed-response questions, the focus is solely on students' understanding of the text, not on their ability to write well. Also, scoring takes into account the possibility of various interpretations that may be acceptable, given appropriate textual support. Consequently, a wide range of answers and writing ability may appear in the responses that receive full credit to any one question.

Score Points

In developing the PIRLS and PIRLS Literacy assessments, the aim is to create blocks of passages and items that each provide, on average, at least 15 score points consisting of the following: approximately seven multiple-choice items (1 point each), two or three short-answer items (1 or 2 points each), and one extended-response item (3 points). Items in each block should address the full range of PIRLS comprehension processes. The exact number of score points and the exact distribution of question types per block will vary somewhat, because different texts yield different types of questions.

The PIRLS Literacy items use multiple-choice and constructed-response formats, as in PIRLS, though constructed-response items usually are worth only one or two points. However, there is a slightly higher percentage of constructed-response items in the PIRLS Literacy assessment, comprising up to 60 percent of the total score points. This decision was made because constructed-response items that require a very short response often are easier for early readers due to the lighter reading demand, as compared with multiple-choice items that require students to read and evaluate four response options. In addition, multiple-choice items may lose some of their effectiveness in passages as short as those used in PIRLS Literacy, because there are fewer plausible distracters that can be drawn from the text.

Releasing Assessment Materials to the Public

An essential aspect of the PIRLS design for measuring trends in reading achievement over time is that, with each cycle, PIRLS releases a number of passages and items into the public domain in order to help readers understand as much as possible about the content and approach of the assessment. At the same time, a number of passages and items are retained and kept confidential to be used in future assessments as the basis for measuring trends. As passages and items are released, new assessment materials are developed to take their place.

According to the PIRLS design, four blocks were released following the PIRLS 2011 data collection, two developed originally for the 2006 assessment, and two from the four developed for 2011. These released passages and items may be found in the *PIRLS 2011 International Results in Reading* (Mullis, Martin, Foy, & Drucker, 2012). Following the publication of the international report for PIRLS 2016, a further six blocks will be released: four that were used in both the 2011 and 2016 assessments, and two from those developed specifically for PIRLS 2016. Additionally, the two PIRLS passages that were included in the PIRLS Literacy booklet design will be released, along with two PIRLS Literacy blocks from 2011 and two from 2016.

ePIRLS 2016 Design

The ePIRLS computer-based assessment of online reading is designed as an extension to PIRLS that measures student informational reading in an online environment. ePIRLS is administered by computer, and requires students to use a mouse or other pointing device to navigate through the assessment and to use a computer keyboard to type their responses to the assessment questions. All students participating in ePIRLS also are expected to have participated in PIRLS. The complete ePIRLS assessment consists of four[3] school-based online reading tasks, each of which involves 2–3 different websites totaling 5 to 10 web pages, together with a series of comprehension questions based on the task. Similar to the PIRLS and PIRLS Literacy passages, each task with accompanying questions takes 40 minutes to complete. In order to keep student response burden to a reasonable level, each individual student completes just two ePIRLS tasks, followed by 5 minutes for a short online questionnaire.

Because ePIRLS is administered by computer, it has greater flexibility than paper-based PIRLS in how the assessment tasks are paired for presentation to

---

[3] Depending on the results of the ePIRLS field test, the number of assessment tasks may be increased to five or six. In that case, the matrix sampling design for task combinations will be extended. In general, if there are n tasks, the number of task combinations is n^2-n.

students. With each student taking two of the four assessment tasks, there are 12 possible task combinations based on task pair and order of administration (see Exhibit 7). ePIRLS uses IEA's WinW3S sampling software to randomly distribute all 12 task combinations across participating students so that approximately 1/12 of the student sample in each country responds to each task combination and these groups of students are approximately equivalent in terms of student ability.

Exhibit 7: ePIRLS 2016 Student Task Combinations—4 Tasks

Student Task Combination	First Task	Second Task
Task Combination #1	E01	E02
Task Combination #2	E01	E03
Task Combination #3	E01	E04
Task Combination #4	E02	E01
Task Combination #5	E02	E03
Task Combination #6	E02	E04
Task Combination #7	E03	E01
Task Combination #8	E03	E02
Task Combination #9	E03	E04
Task Combination #10	E04	E01
Task Combination #11	E04	E02
Task Combination #12	E04	E03

ePIRLS uses item response theory scaling methods to assemble a comprehensive picture of the online informational reading achievement of a country's fourth grade student population by pooling individual students' responses to the tasks that they have been assigned.

Because 2016 is the inaugural year for ePIRLS, all tasks are newly developed. After the 2016 assessment, two of the tasks will be released to the public and the remainder kept secure in order to measure trends in future ePIRLS assessment cycles.

Context Questionnaires and the PIRLS 2016 Encyclopedia

An important purpose of PIRLS 2016 is to study the home, community, school, and student factors associated with children's reading literacy at the fourth grade. To accomplish this purpose, data about the contexts for learning to read are collected through questionnaires completed by students, as well as their parents, teachers, and principals. In addition, National Research Coordinators provide information on the national and community contexts for learning through the curriculum questionnaire and their country's entry in the *PIRLS 2016 Encyclopedia*. Because PIRLS and PIRLS Literacy are reported together in order to assess students in their fourth year of schooling, the same set of questionnaires is used for all students.

PIRLS focuses on policy relevant topics that are generally considered to have a positive relationship with student achievement. Chapter 2 provides an overview of these topics and serves as the basis for item development. Many of the topics are measured through the use of scales—sets of items that measure the same construct. For purposes of reporting, scales are preferable over stand-alone items because they are generally more reliable and more suitable for trend measurement. For PIRLS 2011, 19 scales were reported using context questionnaire data, ranging from measures of parental attitude toward reading to measures of school climate.

Learning to Read Survey (Home Questionnaire)

The Home Questionnaire, entitled the *Learning to Read Survey*, is addressed to the parents or primary caregivers of each student taking part in the PIRLS 2016 data collection. This short questionnaire solicits information on the home context, such as languages spoken in the home, parents' reading activities and attitudes toward reading, and parents' education and occupation. The questionnaire also collects data on the students' educational activities and experiences outside of school including early childhood education, early literacy and numeracy activities, and the child's reading readiness at the beginning of primary school. This questionnaire is designed to take 10–15 minutes to complete.

Teacher Questionnaire

Students' reading teachers are asked to complete this questionnaire, which is designed to gather information about classroom contexts for reading instruction, such as characteristics of the class, reading instructional time, and instructional approaches. The questionnaire also asks about teacher characteristics, such as their career satisfaction, education, and recent professional development activities. This questionnaire requires about 35 minutes to complete.

School Questionnaire

The principal of each school is asked about school characteristics, such as student demographics, the school environment, and the availability of school resources and technology. The questionnaire also includes items focusing on the principal's leadership role, education, and experience. It is designed to take about 30 minutes.

Student Questionnaire

This questionnaire, given to each student once they have completed the reading assessment, collects information on students' home environment, such as languages spoken at home, books in the home, and other home resources for learning. This questionnaire also gathers information on student experiences in school, including feelings of school belonging and whether they are victims of bullying. Finally, the student questionnaire gathers data on out-of-school reading habits and attitudes toward reading, including whether they like reading, their confidence in reading, and their engagement in reading lessons. The student questionnaire requires 15–30 minutes to complete.

ePIRLS Student Questionnaire

In addition to the four questionnaires listed above, students also participating in ePIRLS complete a brief questionnaire as part of this computer-based assessment. The questionnaire asks students about their level of competency and experience using computers and finding information on the Internet. This questionnaire requires 5 minutes to complete.

PIRLS Encyclopedia

The *PIRLS 2016 Encyclopedia* profiles each country's education system, with a particular focus on reading education for primary school children. Each chapter provides an overview of the language/reading curriculum, as well as information on reading instruction in the primary grades. Each chapter also includes information on the languages of instruction, teachers and teacher education, how the education system is organized, and assessment policies. In addition, each chapter provides information on the impact and use of PIRLS in the respective country.

Curriculum Questionnaire

The curriculum questionnaire complements the *PIRLS 2016 Encyclopedia* entries by collecting information from all countries about their national policies on reading curricula, goals and standards for reading instruction, and time specified for reading instruction, as well as information on preprimary education and teacher education policies.

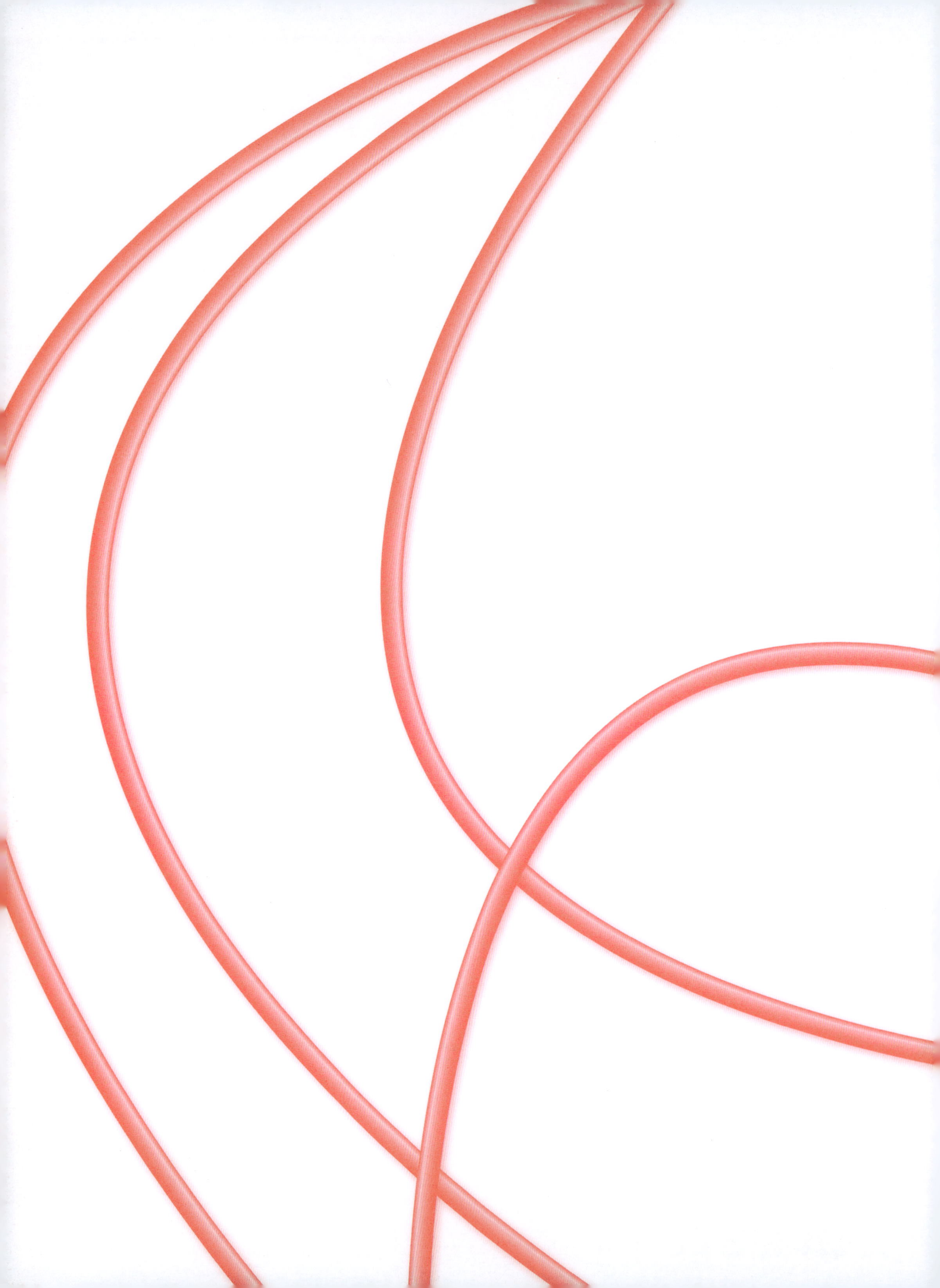

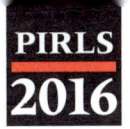

References

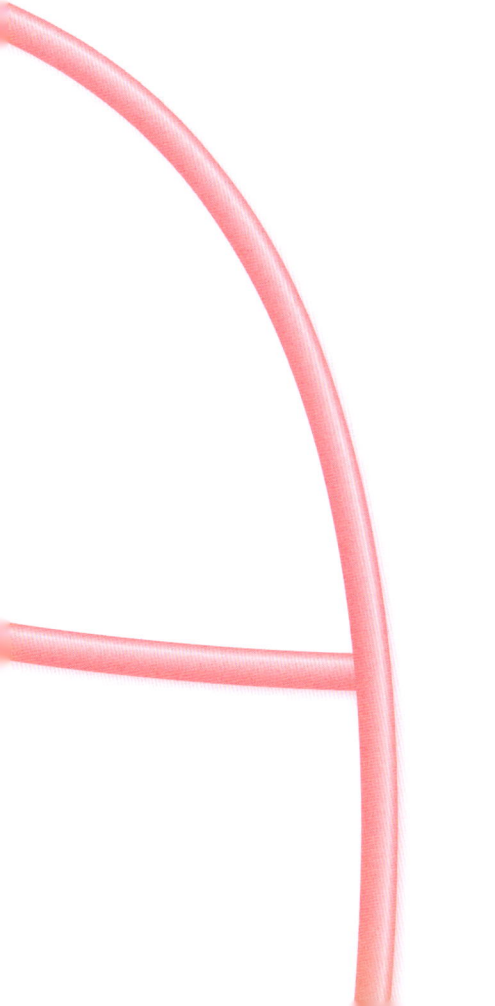

Abedi, J. (2002). Standardized achievement tests and English language learners: Psychometrics issues. *Educational Assessment, 8*(3), 231–257.

Afflerbach, P. & Cho, B. (2009). Identifying and describing constructively responsive comprehension strategies in new and traditional forms of reading. In S. Israel & G. Duffy (Eds.), *Handbook of research on reading comprehension* (pp. 69–90). New York: Routledge.

Agirdag, O., Van Houtte, M., & Van Avermaet, P. (2012). Why does the ethnic and socio-economic composition of schools influence math achievement? The role of sense of futility and futility culture. *European Sociological Review, 28*(3), 366–378.

Akiba, M., LeTendre, G.K., & Scribner, J.P. (2007). Teacher quality, opportunity gap, and national achievement in 46 countries. *Educational Researcher, 36*(7), 369–387.

Alexander, P. & Jetton, T. (2000). Learning from text: A multidimensional and developmental perspective. In M. Kamil, P. Mosenthal, P. Pearson, & R. Barr (Eds.), *Handbook of reading research* (Vol. 3, pp. 285–310). Mahwah, NJ: Lawrence Erlbaum Associates.

Allington, R.L., Mcgill-Franzen, A., Camilli, G., Williams, L., Graff, J., Zeig, J., Zmach, C., & Nowak, R. (2010). Addressing summer reading setback among economically disadvantaged elementary students. *Reading Psychology, 31*(5), 411–427.

Almasi, J. & Garas-York, K. (2009). Comprehension and discussion of text. In S. Israel & G. Duffy (Eds.), *Handbook of research on reading comprehension* (pp. 470–493). New York: Routledge.

Alvermann, D. & Moje, E. (2013). Adolescent literacy instruction and the discourse of "every teacher a teacher of reading." In D. Alvermann, N. Unrau, & R. Ruddell (Eds.), *Theoretical models and processes of reading* (pp. 1072–1103). Newark, DE: International Reading Association.

Anderson, R. & Pearson, P. (1984). A schema-theoretic view of basic processes in reading comprehension. In P. Pearson (Ed.), *Handbook of reading research* (pp. 255–291). White Plains, NY: Longman.

Anmarkrud, Ø. & Bråten, I. (2009). Motivation for reading comprehension. *Learning and Individual Differences, 19*(2), 252–256.

Applebee, A.N., Langer, J.A., Nystrand, M., & Gamoran, A. (2003). Discussion-based approaches to developing understanding: Classroom instruction and student performance in middle and high school English. *American Educational Research Journal, 40*(3), 685–730.

Australian Primary Principals' Association (APPA). (2007). *Experiences of beginning teachers.* Canberra: Author.

Baker, D.P., Akiba, M., LeTendre, G.K., & Wiseman, A.W. (2001). Worldwide shadow education: Outside-school learning, institutional quality of schooling, and cross-national mathematics achievement. *Educational Evaluation and Policy Analysis, 23*(1), 1–17.

Baker, D.P. & LeTendre, G.K. (2005). *National differences, global similarities: World culture and the future of schooling.* Stanford, CA: Stanford University Press.

Baker, L. (2003). The role of parents in motivating struggling readers. *Reading & Writing Quarterly, 19*(1), 87–106.

Baker, L. & Beall, L. (2009). Metacognitive processes and reading comprehension. In S. Israel & G. Duffy (Eds.), *Handbook of research on reading comprehension* (pp. 373–388). New York: Routledge.

Baker, L. & Scher, D. (2002). Beginning readers' motivation for reading in relation to parental beliefs and home reading experiences. *Reading Psychology, 23*(4), 239–269.

Bandura, A. (1997). *Self-efficacy: The exercise of control.* New York: W.H. Freeman and Company.

Başol, G. & Johanson, G. (2009). Effectiveness of frequent testing over achievement: A meta analysis study. *International Journal of Human Sciences, 6*(2), 99–121.

Bawden, D. (2008). Origins and concepts of digital literacy. In C. Lankshear & M. Knobel (Eds.), *Digital literacies: Policies and Practices* (pp. 17–32). New York: Peter Lang Publishing, Inc.

Beach, R. & Hynds, S. (1996). Research on response to literature. In R. Barr, M.L. Kamil, P. Mosenthal, & P.D. Pearson (Eds.), *Handbook of reading research* (Vol. 2, pp. 453–489). Mahwah, NJ: Lawrence Erlbaum Associates.

Becker, M., McElvany, N., & Kortenbruck, M. (2010). Intrinsic and extrinsic reading motivation as predictors of reading literacy: A longitudinal study. *Journal of Educational Psychology, 102*(4), 773–785.

Berlinski, S., Galiani, S., & Gertler, P. (2009). The effect of pre-primary education on primary school performance. *Journal of Public Economics, 93*(1–2), 219–234.

Bialystok, E. (2006). Second-language acquisition and bilingualism at an early age and the impact on early cognitive development. In R.E. Tremblay, M. Boivin, & R.D. Peters (Eds.), *Encyclopedia on early childhood development* [online]. Montreal, Quebec: Centre of Excellence for Early Childhood Development and the Strategic Knowledge Cluster on ECD. Retrieved from http://child-encyclopedia.com/pages/PDF/BialystokANGxp_rev.pdf

Bill & Melinda Gates Foundation. (2013). *Ensuring fair and reliable measures of effective teaching: Culminating findings from the MET project's three-year study.* Retrieved from http://www.metproject.org/downloads/MET_Ensuring_Fair_and_Reliable_Measures_Practitioner_Brief.pdf

Bishop, J.H. & Wößmann, L. (2004). Institutional effects in a simple model of educational production. *Education Economics, 12*(1), 17–38.

Blank, R.K. & de las Alas, N. (2009). *Effects of teacher professional development on gains in student achievement. How meta analysis provides scientific evidence useful to education leaders.* Washington, DC: Council of Chief State School Officers.

Bradley, R.H. & Corwyn, R.F. (2002). Socioeconomic status and child development. *Annual Review of Psychology, 53*(1), 371–399.

Bray, M. (1999). *The shadow education system: Private tutoring and its implications for planners.* Paris: UNESCO, International Institute for Education Planning.

Britt, M., Goldman, S., & Rouet, J. (Eds.). (2012). *Reading: From words to multiple texts.* New York: Routledge.

Britt, M. & Rouet, J. (2012). Learning with multiple documents: Component skills and their acquisition. In M. Lawson & J. Kirby (Eds.), *The quality of learning.* Oxford: Cambridge University Press.

Buchman, C., Condron, D.J., & Roscigno, V.J. (2010). Shadow education, American style: Test preparation, the SAT and college enrollment. *Social Forces, 89*(2), 435–461.

Buckhalt, J.A. (2011). Insufficient sleep and the socioeconomic status achievement gap. *Child Development Perspectives, 5*(1), 59–65.

Campbell, J., Kelly, D., Mullis, I.V.S., Martin, M.O., & Sainsbury, M. (2001). *Framework and specifications for PIRLS assessment 2001, second edition.* Chestnut

Hill, MA: TIMSS & PIRLS International Study Center, Boston College.

Caprara, G.V., Barbaranelli, C., Steca, P., & Malone, P.S. (2006). Teachers' self-efficacy beliefs as determinants of job satisfaction and students' academic achievement: A study at the school level. *Journal of School Psychology, 44*(6), 473–490.

Castek, J., Zawilinski, L., McVerry, G., O'Byrne, I., & Leu, D.J. (2010). The new literacies of online reading comprehension: New opportunities and challenges for students with learning difficulties. In C. Wyatt-Smith, J. Elkins, & S. Gunn (Eds.), *Multiple perspectives on difficulties in learning literacy and numeracy* (pp. 91–110). New York, NY: Springer.

Catsambis, S. & Buttaro, A. (2012). Revisiting "Kindergarten as academic boot camp: A nationwide study of ability grouping and psycho-social development." *Social Psychology of Education, 15*(4), 483–515.

Chall, J. (1983). *Stages of reading development*. New York: McGraw-Hill.

Chiong, C. & Shuler, C. (2010). *Learning: Is there an app for that? Investigations of young children's usage and learning with mobile devices and apps*. New York: The Joan Ganz Cooney Center at Sesame Workshop.

Christianson, K. & Luke, S. (2011). Context strengthens initial misinterpretations of text. *Scientific Studies of Reading, 15*(2), 136–166.

Clark, C. (2010). *Linking school libraries and literacy: Young people's reading habits and attitudes to their school library, and an exploration of the relationship between school library use and school attainment*. London: National Literacy Trust.

Clotfelter, C.T., Ladd, H.F., & Vigdor, J.L. (2010). Teacher credentials and student achievement in high school: A cross-subject analysis with student fixed effects. *The Journal of Human Resources, 45*(3), 655–681.

Cohen, J., McCabe, L., Michelli, N.M., & Pickeral, T. (2009). School climate: Research, policy, practice and teacher education. *Teachers College Record, 111*(1), 180–213.

Coiro, J. (2003). Exploring literacy on the Internet: Reading comprehension on the Internet: Expanding our understanding of reading comprehension to encompass new literacies. *The Reading Teacher, 56*(5), 458–464.

Coiro, J. (2011). Predicting reading comprehension on the Internet: Contributions of offline reading skills, online reading skills and prior knowledge. *Journal of Literacy Research, 43*(4), 352–392.

Coiro, J. (2012). The new literacies of online reading comprehension: Future directions. *The Educational Forum, 76*(4), 412–417.

Coiro, J. & Kennedy, C. (2011, June). *The online reading comprehension assessment (ORCA) project: Preparing students for common core standards and 21st century literacies*. Unpublished manuscript. Kingston, RI: University of Rhode Island. Retrieved from http://www.orca.uconn.edu/orca/assets/File/Research%20Reports/CCSS%20ORCA%20Alignment%20June%202011.pdf

Coleman, J., Campbell, E., Hobson, C., McPartland, J., Mood, A., Weinfeld, F., & York, R. (1966). *Equality of opportunity*. Washington, DC: National Center for Educational Statistics, US Government Printing Office.

Cornelius-White, J. (2007). Learner-centered teacher-student relationships are effective: A meta-analysis. *Review of Educational Research, 77*(1), 113–143.

Coulombe, S., Trembly, J., & Marchand, S. (2004). *Literacy scores, human capital, and growth across fourteen OECD countries*. Ottawa: Statistics Canada.

Croninger, R.G., Rice, J.K., Rathbun, A., & Nishio, M. (2007). Teacher qualifications and early learning: Effects of certification, degree, and experience on first-grade student achievement. *Economics of Education Review, 26*(3), 312–324.

Csikszentmihalyi, M. (1990). *Flow: The psychology of optimal experience*. New York: Harper & Row.

Dahl, G.B. & Lochner, L. (2012). The impact of family income on child achievement: Evidence from the earned income tax credit. *American Economic Review, 102*(5), 1927–1956.

Darling, S. & Westberg, L. (2004). Parent involvement in children's acquisition of reading. *The Reading Teacher, 57*(8), 774–776.

Darling-Hammond, L. (2000). How teacher education matters. *Journal of Teacher Education, 51*(3), 166–173.

Davis-Kean, P.E. (2005). The influence of parent education and family income on child achievement: The indirect role of parental expectations and the home environment. *Journal of Family Psychology, 19*(2), 294–304.

Dearing, E., Kreider, H., & Weiss, H.B. (2008). Increased family involvement in school predicts improved child-teacher relationships and feelings about school for low-income children. *Marriage & Family Review, 43*(3–4), 226–254.

Deci, E.L. & Moller, A.C. (2005). The concept of competence: A starting place for understanding intrinsic motivation and self-determined extrinsic motivation. In A.J. Elliot & C.S. Dweck (Eds.), *Handbook of competence and motivation* (pp. 579–597). New York: Guilford Publications.

Deci, E.L. & Ryan, R.M. (1985). *Intrinsic motivation and self-determination in human behavior*. New York: Plenum Press.

Deci, E.L., Koestner, R., & Ryan, R.M. (1999). A meta-analytic review of experiments examining the effects of extrinsic rewards on intrinsic motivation. *Psychological Bulletin, 125*(6), 627–668.

De Naeghel, J., Van Keer, H., Vansteenkiste, M., & Rosseel, Y. (2012). The relation between elementary students' recreational and academic reading motivation, reading frequency, engagement, and comprehension: A self-determination theory perspective. *Journal of Educational Psychology, 104*(4), 1006–1021.

Dewald, J.F., Meijer, A.M., Oort, F.J., Kerkhof, G.A., & Bögels, S.M. (2010). The influence of sleep quality, sleep duration and sleepiness on school performance in children and adolescents: A meta-analytic review. *Sleep Medicine Reviews, 14*(3), 179–189.

DuFour, R., Eaker, R., & DuFour, R. (2005). Recurring themes of professional learning communities and the assumptions they challenge. In R. DuFour, R. Eaker, & R. DuFour (Eds.), *On common ground: The power of professional learning communities* (pp. 7–29). Bloomington, IN: National Education Service.

Duke, N. (2004). The case for informational text. *Educational Leadership, 61*(6), 40–44.

Duke. N. & Carlisle, J. (2011). The development of comprehension. In M. Kamil, P. D. Pearson, E. Moje, & P. Afflerbach (Eds.), *Handbook of reading research* (Vol. 4, pp. 199–228). New York: Routledge.

Ehri, L.C., Nunes, S.R., Willows, D.M., Shuster, B.V., Yaghoub-Zadeh, Z., & Shanahan, T. (2001). Phonemic awareness instruction helps children learn to read: Evidence from the National Reading Panel's meta-analysis. *Reading Research Quarterly, 36*(3), 250–287.

Elleman, A.M., Lindo, E.J., Morphy, P., & Compton, D.L. (2009). The impact of vocabulary instruction on passage-level comprehension of school-age children: A meta-analysis. *Journal of Research on Educational Effectiveness, 2*(1), 1–44.

Elley, W. (1992). *How in the world do students read?* The Hague, Netherlands: International Association for the Evaluation of Educational Achievement (IEA).

Elley, W. (Ed.). (1994). *The IEA study of reading literacy: Achievement and instruction in thirty-two school systems.* Oxford: Elsevier Science Ltd.

Entorf, H. & Minoiu, N. (2005). What a difference immigration policy makes: A comparison of PISA scores in Europe and traditional countries of immigration. *German Economic Review, 6*(3), 355–376.

Erberber, E. (2009). *Analyzing Turkey's data from TIMSS 2007 to investigate regional disparities in eighth grade science achievement* (Doctoral dissertation, Boston College). Retrieved from http://dcollections.bc.edu/webclient/StreamGate?folder_id=0&dvs=1383662559807~299

Fauth, B., Decristan, J., Rieser, S., Klieme, E., & Büttner, G. (2014). Student ratings of teaching quality in primary school: Dimensions and prediction of student outcomes. *Learning and Instruction, 29,* 1–9.

Federal Interagency Forum on Child and Family Statistics. (2013). *America's children in brief: Key national indicators of well-being, 2013.* Washington, DC: US Government Printing Office.

Flavell, J. & Wellman, H. (Eds.). (1977). *Metamemory.* Hillsdale, NJ: Lawrence Erlbaum Associates.

Foy, P., Brossman, B., & Galia, J. (2012). *Scaling the TIMSS and PIRLS 2011 achievement data.* Chestnut Hill, MA: TIMSS & PIRLS International Study Center at Boston College. Retrieved from http://timssandpirls.bc.edu/methods/pdf/TP11_Scaling_Achievement.pdf

Galda, L. & Beach, R. (2001). Response to literature as a cultural activity. *Reading Research Quarterly, 36*(1), 64–73.

Gambrell, L.B., Malloy, J.A., & Mazzoni, S.A. (2011). Evidence-based best practices in comprehensive literacy instruction. In L.M. Morrow & L.B. Gambrell (Eds.), *Best practices in literacy instruction, fourth edition* (pp. 11–36). New York, NY: Guilford Press.

Glew, G.M., Fan, M., Katon, W., & Rivara, F.P. (2008). Bullying and school safety. *The Journal of Pediatrics, 152*(1), 123–128.

Goddard, Y.L., Goddard, R.D., & Tschannen-Moran, M. (2007). A theoretical and empirical investigation of teacher collaboration for school improvement and student achievement in public elementary schools. *The Teachers College Record, 109*(4), 877–896.

Goldman, S. & Rakestraw, J. Jr. (2000). Structural aspects of constructing meaning from text. In M. Kamil, P. Mosenthal, P. Pearson, & R. Barr (Eds.), *Handbook of reading research* (Vol. 3, pp. 311–336). Mahwah, NJ: Lawrence Erlbaum Associates.

Goodenow, C. & Grady, K.E. (1993). The relationship of school belonging and friends values to academic motivation among urban adolescent students. *Journal of Experimental Education, 62*(1), 60–71.

Goos, M., Schreier, B.M., Knipprath, H.M.E., De Fraine, B., Van Damme, J., & Trautwein, U. (2013). How can cross-country differences in the practice of grade retention be explained? A closer look at national educational policy factors. *Comparative Education Review, 57*(1), 54–84.

Gottfredson, G.D., Gottfredson, D.C., Payne, A.A., & Gottfredson, N.C. (2005). School climate predictors of school disorder: Results from a national study of delinquency prevention in schools. *Journal of Research in Crime and Delinquency, 42*(4), 412–444.

Graesser, A., Golding, J., & Long, D. (1996). Narrative representation and comprehension. In R. Barr, M. Kamil, P. Mosenthal, & P. Pearson (Eds.), *Handbook of reading research* (Vol. 2, pp. 171–205). Mahwah, NJ: Lawrence Erlbaum Associates.

Greenberg, E., Skidmore, D., & Rhodes, D. (2004). *Climates for learning: Mathematics achievement and its relationship to schoolwide student behavior, schoolwide parental involvement, and school morale.* Paper presented at the annual meeting of the American Educational Researchers Association, San Diego, CA.

Greenwald, R., Hedges, L.V., & Laine, R.D. (1996). The effect of school resources on student achievement. *Review of Educational Research, 66*(3), 361–396.

Guarino, C.M., Sanitibañez, L., & Daley, G.A. (2006). Teacher recruitment and retention: A review of the recent empirical literature. *Review of Educational Research, 76*(2), 173–208.

Gustafsson, J.-E., Hansen, K.Y., & Rosén, M. (2013). Effects of home background on student achievement in reading, mathematics, and science at the fourth grade. In M.O. Martin & I.V.S. Mullis (Eds.), *TIMSS and PIRLS 2011: Relationships among reading, mathematics, and science achievement at the fourth grade—Implications for early learning*. Chestnut Hill, MA: TIMSS & PIRLS International Study Center, Boston College.

Guthrie, J. (1996). Educational contexts for engagement in literacy. *The Reading Teacher, 49*(6), 432–445.

Guthrie, J.T., McRae, A., & Klauda, S.L. (2007). Contributions of concept-oriented reading instruction to knowledge about interventions for motivations in reading. *Educational Psychologist, 42*(4), 237–250.

Guthrie, J.T., Wigfield, A., Humenick, N.M., Perencevich, K.C., Taboada, A., & Barbosa, P. (2006). Influences of stimulating tasks on reading motivation and comprehension. *Journal of Educational Research, 99*(4), 232–245.

Gutnick, A.L., Robb, M., Takeuchi, L., & Kotler, J. (2011). *Always connected: The new digital media habits of young children*. New York: The Joan Ganz Cooney Center at Sesame Workshop.

Hancock, C.B. & Sherff, L. (2010). Who will stay and who will leave? Predicting secondary English teacher attrition risk. *Journal of Teacher Education, 61*(4), 328–338.

Harris, D.N. & Sass, T.R. (2011). Teacher training, teacher quality and student achievement. *Journal of Public Economics, 95*(7–8), 798–812.

Hart, B. & Risley, T.R. (2003). The early catastrophe: The 30 million word gap. *American Educator, 27*(1), 4–9.

Hattie, J. (2009). *Visible learning: A synthesis of over 800 meta-analyses relating to achievement.* New York: Routledge.

Henson, R.K. (2002). From adolescent angst to adulthood: Substantive implications and measurement dilemmas in the development of teacher efficacy research. *Educational Psychologist, 37*(3), 137–150.

Hill, H.C., Rowan, B., & Ball, D.L. (2005). Effects of teachers' mathematical knowledge for teaching on student achievement. *American Educational Research Journal, 42*(2), 371–406.

Hill, N.E. & Tyson, D.F. (2009). Parental involvement in middle school: A meta-analytic assessment of the strategies that promote achievement. *Developmental Psychology, 45*(3), 740–763.

Hoff, E. & Elledge, C. (2005). Bilingualism as one of many environmental variables that affect language development. In J. Cohen, K.T. McAlister, K. Rolstad, & J. MacSwan (Eds.), *Proceedings of the 4th International Symposium on Bilingualism* (pp. 1041–1044). Somerville, MA: Cascadilla Press.

Hong, S. & Ho, H.-Z. (2005). Direct and indirect longitudinal effects of parental involvement on student achievement: Second-order latent growth modeling across ethnic groups. *Journal of Educational Psychology, 97*(1), 32–42.

Hoy, W.K., Tarter, C.J., & Hoy, A.W. (2006). Academic optimism of schools: A force for student achievement. *American Educational Research Journal, 43*(3), 425–446.

Hsu, H.-Y., Wang, S.-K., & Runco, L. (2013). Middle school science teachers' confidence and pedagogical practice of new literacies. *Journal of Science Education and Technology, 22*(3), 314–324.

Jeynes, W.H. (2005). A meta-analysis of the relation of parental involvement to urban elementary school student academic achievement. *Urban Education, 40*(3), 237–269.

Jeynes, W.H. (2007). The relationship between parental involvement and urban secondary school student academic achievement: A meta-analysis. *Urban Education, 42*(1), 82–110.

Jimerson, S.R. (2001). Meta-analysis of grade retention research: Implications for practice in the 21st century. *School Psychology Review, 30*(3), 420–437.

Johansone, I. (2009). *Managing primary education in Latvia to assure quality and achievement equity* (Doctoral dissertation, University of Latvia).

Johnson, S.M. (2006). *The workplace matters: Teacher quality, retention and effectiveness*. Washington, DC: National Education Association.

Johnson, S.M., Berg, J.H., & Donaldson, M.L. (2005). *Who stays in teaching and why: A review of the literature on teacher retention*. Cambridge, MA: Harvard Graduate School of Education.

Johnson, S.M., Kraft, M.A., & Papay, J.P. (2012). How context matters in high-need schools: The effects of teachers' working conditions on their professional satisfaction and their students' achievement. *Teachers College Record, 114*(10), 1–39.

Jürges, H., Schneider, K., & Büchel, F. (2005). The effect of central exit examinations on student achievement: Quasi-experimental evidence from TIMSS Germany. *Journal of the European Economic Association, 3*(5), 1134–1155.

Kim, J.S. & Quinn, D.M. (2013). The effects of summer reading on low-income children's literacy achievement from Kindergarten to Grade 8: A meta-analysis of classroom and home interventions. *Review of Educational Research, 83*(3), 386–431.

Kintsch, W. (1998). *Comprehension: A paradigm for cognition*. New York: Cambridge University Press.

Kintsch, W. (2012). Psychological models of reading comprehension and their implications for assessments. In J. Sabatini, E. Albro, & T. O'Reilly (Eds.), *Measuring up: Advances in how to assess reading ability* (pp. 21–37). Plymouth, UK: Rowman & Littlefield Publishers.

Kintsch, W. (2013). Revisiting the construction-integration model of text comprehension and its implications for Instruction. In D. Alvermann, N. Unrau, & R. Ruddell (Eds.), *Theoretical models and processes of reading* (pp. 807–841). Newark, DE: International Reading Association.

Kintsch, W. & Kintsch, E. (2005). Comprehension. In S. Paris & S. Stahl (Eds.), *Children's reading comprehension and assessment* (pp. 71–92). Mahwah, NJ: Lawrence Erlbaum Associates.

Klauda, S.L. & Wigfield, A. (2012). Relations of perceived parent and friend support for recreational reading with children's reading motivations. *Journal of Literacy Research, 44*(1), 3–44.

Klein, H.J., Wesson, M.J., Hollenbeck, J.R., & Alge, B.J. (1999). Goal commitment and the goal-setting process: Conceptual clarification and empirical synthesis. *Journal of Applied Psychology, 84*(6), 885–896.

Klieme, E., Pauli, C., & Reusser, K. (2009). The Pythagoras study—Investigating effects of teaching and learning in Swiss and German mathematics classrooms. In T. Janik & T. Seidel (Eds.), *The power of video studies in investigating teaching and learning in the classroom*. (pp. 137–160). Münster: Waxmann.

Kloosterman, R., Notten, N., Tolsma, J., & Kraaykamp, G. (2010). The effects of parental reading socialization and early school involvement on children's academic performance: A panel study of primary school pupils in the Netherlands. *European Sociological Review, 27*(3), 291–306.

Kobayashi, M. (2002). Method effects on reading comprehension test performance: Text organization and response format. *Language Testing, 19*(2), 193–220.

Konishi, C., Hymel, S., Zumbo, B.D., & Li, Z. (2010). Do school bullying and student-teacher relationships matter for academic achievement? A multilevel analysis. *Journal of School Psychology, 25*(1), 19–39.

Kucer, S. (2005). *Dimensions of literacy: A conceptual base for teaching reading and writing in school settings, second edition*. Mahwah, NJ: Lawrence Erlbaum Associates.

Langer, J. (2011). *Envisioning literature, second edition*. Newark, DE: International Reading Association.

Lee, J.-W. & Barro, R.J. (2001). Schooling quality in a cross-section of countries. *Economica, New Series, 68*(272), 465–488.

Lee, S.M., Brescia, W., & Kissinger, D. (2009). Computer use and academic development in secondary schools. *Computers in the Schools, 26*(3), 224–235.

Lee, V.E. & Zuze, T.L. (2011). School resources and academic performance in Sub-Saharan Africa. *Comparative Education Review, 55*(3), 369–397.

Leigh, A.K. (2010). Estimating teacher effectiveness from two-year changes in students' test scores. *Economics of Education Review, 29*(3), 480–488.

Leppänen, U., Aunola, K., & Nurmi, J.-E. (2005). Beginning readers' reading performance and reading habits. *Journal of Research in Reading, 28*(4), 383–399.

Leu, D., Kinzer, C., Coiro, J., & Cammack, D. (2004). Toward a theory of new literacies emerging from the internet and other information and communication technologies. In R.B. Ruddell & N.J. Unrau (Eds.), *Theoretical models and processes of reading, fifth edition* (pp. 1570–1613). Newark, DE: International Reading Association.

Leu, D., Kinzer, C., Coiro, J., Castek, J., & Henry, L. (2013). New literacies: A dual level theory of the changing nature of literacy, instruction and assessment. In D. Alvermann, N. Unrau, & R. Ruddell (Eds.), *Theoretical models and processes of reading, sixth edition* (pp. 1150–1181). Newark, DE: International Reading Association.

Leu, D., Kulikowich, J., Sedansk, N., & Coiro, J. (2008). Framework document: The new literacies of online research and comprehension. In *Assessing online reading comprehension: The ORCA project*. A grant proposal to the US Department of Education, Institute of Education Sciences.

Leu, D., Mcverry, J.G., O'Byrne, W.I., Zawilinski, L., Castek, J., & Hartman, D.K. (2009). The new literacies of online reading comprehension and the irony of No Child Left Behind. In L.M. Morrow, R. Rueda, & D. Lapp (Eds.), *Handbook of research on literacy and diversity* (pp. 173–194). New York: The Guilford Press.

Leu, D., O'Byrne, W., Zawilinski, L., McVerry, J., & Everett-Cacopardo, H. (2009). Expanding the new literacies conversation. *Educational Researcher, 38*(4), 264–269.

Leu, D.J., Zawilinski, L., Castek, J., Banerjee, M., Housand, B.C., Liu, Y., & O'Neil, M. (2007). What is new about the new literacies of online reading comprehension? In L.S. Rush, A.J. Eakle, & A. Berger (Eds.), *Secondary school literacy: What research reveals for classroom practices* (pp. 37–68). Urbana, IL: National Council of Teachers of English.

Lewis, M. & Samuels, S.J. (2003). *Read more—Read better? A meta-analysis of the literature on the relationship between exposure to reading and reading achievement*. University of Minnesota, Minneapolis, MN. Retrieved from http://www.tc.umn.edu/~samue001/final%20version.pdf

Lieberman, D.A., Bates, C.H., & So, J. (2009). Young children's learning with digital media. *Computers in the Schools, 26*(4), 271–283.

Lipowsky, F., Rakoczy, K., Pauli, C., Drollinger-Vetter, B., Klieme, E., & Reusser, K. (2009). Quality of geometry instruction and its short-term impact on students' understanding of the Pythagorean Theorem. *Learning and Instruction, 19*(6), 527–537.

Lleras, C. & Rangel, C. (2009). Ability grouping practices in elementary school and African-American/Hispanic achievement. *American Journal of Education, 115*(2), 279–304.

Logan, S., Medford, E., & Hughes, N. (2011). The importance of intrinsic motivation for high and low ability readers' reading comprehension performance. *Learning and Individual Differences, 21*(1), 124–128.

Lorch, R., Lemarie, J., & Grant, R. (2011). Signaling hierarchical and sequential organization in expository prose. *Scientific Studies of Reading, 15*(3), 267–284.

Lou, Y, Abrami, P.C., & Spence, J.C. (2000). Effects of within-class grouping on student achievement: An exploratory model. *The Journal of Educational Research, 94*(2), 101–112.

Lou, Y., Abrami, P.C., Spence, J.C., Poulsen, C., Chambers, B., & d'Apollonia, S. (1996). Within-class grouping: a metaanalysis. *Review of Educational Research, 66*(4), 423–458.

Marsh, H.W. & Craven, R.G. (2006). Reciprocal effects of self-concept and performance from a multidimensional perspective: Beyond seductive pleasure and unidimensional perspectives. *Perspectives on Psychological Science, 1*(2), 133–163.

Martin, A.J. (2006). Personal bests (PBs): A proposed multidimensional model and empirical analysis. *British Journal of Educational Psychology, 76*(4), 803–825.

Martin, M.O., Foy, P., Mullis, I.V.S., & O'Dwyer, L.M. (2013). Effective schools in reading, mathematics, and science at the fourth grade. In M.O. Martin & I.V.S. Mullis (Eds.), *TIMSS and PIRLS 2011: Relationships among reading, mathematics, and science achievement at the fourth grade—Implications for early learning*. Chestnut Hill, MA: TIMSS & PIRLS International Study Center, Boston College.

Martin, M.O. & Mullis, I.V.S. (Eds.). (2013). *TIMSS and PIRLS 2011: Relationships among reading, mathematics, and science achievement at the fourth grade—Implications for early learning.* Chestnut Hill, MA: TIMSS & PIRLS International Study Center, Boston College.

Martin, M.O., Mullis, I.V.S., & Foy, P. (2011). Age distribution and reading achievement configurations among fourth-grade students in PIRLS 2006. *IERI Monograph Series: Issues and Methodologies in Large-scale Assessments, 4,* 9–33.

Marzano, R.J., Marzano, J.S., & Pickering, D.J. (2003). *Classroom management that works: Research-based strategies for every teacher.* Alexandria, VA: Association of Supervision and Curriculum Development.

McGuigan, L. & Hoy, W.K. (2006). Principal leadership: Creating a culture of academic optimism to improve achievement for all students. *Leadership and Policy in Schools, 5*(3), 203–229.

McLaughlin, M., Mc.Grath, D.J., Burian-Fitzgerald, M.A., Lanahan, L., Scotchmer, M., Enyeart, C., & Salganik, L. (2005, April). *Student content engagement as a construct for the measurement of effective classroom instruction and teacher knowledge.* Paper presented at the annual meeting of the American Educational Researchers Association, Montreal, Canada.

Melhuish, E.C., Phan, M.B., Sylva, K., Sammons, P., Siraj-Blatchford, I., & Taggert, B. (2008). Effects of the home learning environment and preschool center experience upon literacy and numeracy development in early primary school. *Journal of Social Issues, 64*(1), 95–114.

Milam, A.J., Furr-Holden, C.D.M., & Leaf, P.J. (2010). Perceived school and neighborhood safety, neighborhood violence and academic achievement in urban school children. *The Urban Review, 42*(5), 458–467.

Miller, S. & Faircloth, B. (2009). Motivation and reading comprehension. In S. Israel & G. Duffy (Eds.), *Handbook of research on reading comprehension* (pp. 227–239). New York: Routledge.

Mishna, F., Cook, C., Gadalla, T., Daciuk, J., & Solomon, S. (2010). Cyber bullying behaviors among middle and high school students. *American Journal of Orthopsychiatry, 80*(3), 363–374.

Mol, S.E. & Bus, A.G. (2011). To read or not to read: A meta-analysis of print exposure from infancy to adulthood. *Psychological Bulletin, 137*(2), 267–296.

Morrow, L. (2003). Motivating lifelong voluntary readers. In J. Flood, D. Lapp, J.R. Squire, & J.M. Jenson (Eds.), *Handbook of teaching the English language arts, second edition* (pp. 857–867). Hillsdale, NJ: Lawrence Erlbaum Associates, Inc.

Moskowitz, J. & Stephens, M. (Eds.). (1997). *From students of teaching to teachers of students: Teacher induction around the Pacific rim.* Washington, DC: US Department of Education.

Mueller, J., Wood, E., Willoughby, T., Ross, C., & Specht, J. (2008). Identifying discriminating variables between teachers who fully integrate computers and teachers with limited integration. *Computers & Education, 51*(4), 1523–1537.

Mullis, I.V.S., Kennedy, A., Martin, M.O., & Sainsbury, M. (2006). *PIRLS 2006 assessment framework and specifications, second edition.* Chestnut Hill, MA: TIMSS & PIRLS International Study Center, Boston College.

Mullis, I.V.S., Martin, M.O., Foy, P., & Drucker, K.T. (2012). *PIRLS 2011 international results in reading.* Chestnut Hill, MA: TIMSS & PIRLS International Study Center, Boston College.

Mullis, I.V.S., Martin, M.O., Kennedy, A., Trong, K., & Sainsbury, M. (2009). *PIRLS 2011 assessment framework*. Chestnut Hill, MA: TIMSS & PIRLS International Study Center, Boston College.

Mullis, I.V.S., Martin, M.O., Minnich, C.A., Drucker, K.T., & Ragan, M.A. (Eds.). (2012). *PIRLS 2011 encyclopedia: Education policy and curriculum in reading (Volume 1 & 2)*. Chestnut Hill, MA: TIMSS & PIRLS International Study Center, Boston College.

Murphy, P.K., Wilkinson, I.A., Soter, A.O., Hennessey, M.N., & Alexander, J.F. (2009). Examining the effects of classroom discussion on students' comprehension of text: A meta-analysis. *Journal of Educational Psychology, 101*(3), 740–764.

Murnane, R., Sawhill, I., & Snow, C. (2012). Literacy challenges for the twenty-first century: Introducing the issue. *The Future of Children, 22*(2), 3–15.

Murphy, P., Wilkinson, I., Soter, A., Hennessey, M., & Alexander, J. (2009). Examining the effects of classroom discussion on students' comprehension of text: A meta-analysis. *Journal of Educational Psychology, 101*(3), 740–764.

Nesbit, J.C. & Adesope, O.O. (2006). Learning with concept and knowledge maps: A meta-analysis. *Review of Educational Research, 76*(3), 413–448.

Niemiec, C.P. & Ryan, R.M. (2009). Autonomy, competence, and relatedness in the classroom: Applying self-determination theory to educational practice. *Theory and Research in Education, 7*(2), 133–144.

Organisation for Economic Cooperation and Development. (1995). *Literacy, economy and society*. Paris: Author.

Organisation for Economic Cooperation and Development. (1997). *Literacy skills for knowledge society: Further results from the international adult literacy survey*. Paris: Author.

Organisation for Economic Cooperation and Development. (2001). *Knowledge and skills for life: First results from the OECD programme for international student assessment (PISA) 2000*. Paris: Author.

Organisation for Economic Cooperation and Development. (2010). *Improving health and social cohesion through education*. Paris: Author.

Organisation for Economic Cooperation and Development, with Statistics Canada. (2000). *Literacy in the information age: Final report of the international adult literacy survey*. Paris: Author/Statistics Canada.

Organisation for Economic Cooperation and Development, with Statistics Canada. (2005). *Learning a living: First results of the adult literacy and life skills survey*. Paris and Ottawa: Author/Statistics Canada.

Palincsar, A. & Duke, N. (2004). The role of text and text-reader interactions in young children's reading development and achievement. *The Elementary School Journal, 105*(2), 183–197.

Paris, S.G., Wasik, B.A., & Turner, J.C. (1996). The development of strategic readers. In R. Barr, M.L. Kamil, P. Mosenthal, & P.D. Pearson (Eds.), *Handbook of reading research* (Vol. 2, pp. 609–640). Mahwah, NJ: Lawrence Erlbaum Associates.

Perfetti, C. (2007). Reading ability: Lexical quality to comprehension. *Scientific Studies of Reading, 11*(4), 357–383.

Perfetti, C. & Adolf, S. (2012). Reading comprehension: A conceptual framework from word meaning to text meaning. In J. Sabatini, E. Albro, & T. O'Reilly (Eds.), *Measuring up: Advances in how to assess reading ability*. Lanham, MD: Rowman & Littlefield.

Perfitti, C., Landi, N., & Oakhill, J. (2005). The acquisition of reading comprehension skills. In M.J. Snowling & C. Hulme (Eds.), *The science of reading: A handbook* (pp. 227–247). Malden, MA: Blackwell Publishing.

Perkinson-Gloor, N., Lemola, S., & Grob, A. (2013). Sleep duration, positive attitude toward life, and academic achievement: The role of daytime tiredness, behavioral persistence, and school start times. *Journal of Adolescence, 36*(2), 311–318.

Pew Research Center. (2012). *How teens do research in the digital world*. Washington, DC: Author.

Pew Research Center. (2013a). *Teens and technology*. Washington, DC: Author.

Pew Research Center. (2013b). *How teachers are using technology at home and in the classrooms*. Washington, DC: Author.

Pressley, M. (2002). Metacognition and self-regulated comprehension. In A.E. Farstrup & J.S. Samuels (Eds.), *What research has to say about reading instruction, third edition* (pp. 291–309). Newark, DE: International Reading Association.

Pressley, M. & Gaskins, I. (2006). Metacognitively competent reading comprehension is constructively responsive reading: How can such reading be developed in students? *Metacognition Learning, 1*(1), 99–113.

Puzio, K. & Colby, G. (2010). *The effects of within class grouping on reading achievement: A meta-analytic synthesis*. Evanston, IL: Society for Research on Educational Effectiveness. Retrieved from ERIC database (ED514135).

Raikes, H., Pan, B.A., Luze, G., Tamis-LeMonda, C.S., Brooks-Gunn, J., Constantine, J., Tarullo, L.B., Raikes, H.A., & Rodriguez, E.T. (2006). Mother–child bookreading in low-income families: Correlates and outcomes during the first three years of life. *Child Development, 77*(4), 924–953.

Rapp, D. & van den Broek, P. (2005). Dynamic text comprehension: An integrative view of reading. *Current Directions in Psychological Science, 14*(5), 276–279.

Reeve, J., Jang, H., Carrell, D., Jeon, S., & Barch, J. (2004). Enhancing students' engagement by increasing teachers autonomy support. *Motivation and Emotion, 28*(2), 147–169.

Reuda, R. (2013). 21st-century skills: Cultural, linguistic, and motivational perspectives. In D. Alvermann, N. Unrau, & R. Ruddell (Eds.), *Theoretical models and processes of reading, sixth edition* (pp. 1241–1268). Newark, DE: International Reading Association.

Rideout, V.J., Foehr, U.G., & Roberts, D.F. (2010). *Generation M2. Media in the lives of 8- to 18-year-olds.* Menlo Park, CA: The Kaiser Family Foundation.

Robinson, V.M.J., Lloyd, C.A., & Rowe, K.J. (2008). The impact of leadership on student outcomes: An analysis of the differential effects of leadership types. *Educational Administration Quarterly, 44*(5), 635–674.

Rosell, J. & Pahl, K. (2010). The materials and the situated: What multimodality and new literacy studies do for literacy research. In D. Lapp & D. Fisher (Eds.), *Handbook of research on teaching the English language arts, third edition* (pp. 1462–1521). Newark, DE: International Reading Association.

Rothon, C., Head, J., Klineberg, E., & Stansfeld, S. (2011). Can social support protect bullied adolescents from adverse outcomes? A prospective study on the effects of bullying on the educational achievement and mental health of adolescents at secondary schools in East London. *Journal of Adolescence, 34*(3), 579–588.

Routman, R. (2003). *Reading essentials: The specifics you need to teach reading well*. Portsmouth, NH: Heinemann.

Rowsell, J., Kress, G., Pahl, K., & Street, B. (2013). The social practice of multimodal reading: A new literacy studies—multimodal perspective on reading. In D. Alvermann, N. Unrau, & R. Ruddell (Eds.), *Theoretical models and processes of reading, sixth edition* (pp. 1182–1207). Newark, DE: International Reading Association.

Ruddell, R. & Unrau, N. (Eds.). (2004). Read as a meaning-construction process: The reader, the text, and the teacher. In R. Ruddell & N. Unrau (Eds.), *Theoretical models and processes of reading, fifth edition* (pp. 1462–1521). Newark, DE: International Reading Association.

Rumberger, R.W. & Palardy, G.J. (2005). Does segregation still matter? The impact of student composition on academic achievement in high school. *The Teachers College Record, 107*(9), 1999–2045.

Rumelhart, D. (1985). Toward an interactive model of reading. In H. Singer & R. Ruddell (Eds.), *Theoretical models and the processes of reading, third edition* (pp. 722–750). Newark, DE: International Reading Association.

Russell, M., Bebell, D., O'Dwyer, L., & O'Connor, K. (2003). Examining teacher technology use: Implications for preservice and inservice teacher preparation. *Journal of Teacher Education, 54*(4), 297–310.

Ryan, R.M. & Deci, E.L. (2000). Self-determination theory and the facilitation of intrinsic motivation, social development, and well-being. *American Psychologist, 55*(1), 68–78.

Sammons, P., Sylva, K., Melhuish, E.C., Siraj-Blatchford, I., Taggart, B., & Elliot, K. (2002). *The effective provision of pre-school education (EPPE) project: Measuring the impact of pre-school on children's cognitive progress over the pre-school period* (Technical Paper No. 8a). London: Institute of Education, University of London/Department for Education and Skills.

Schiefele, U., Schaffner, E., Möller, J., & Wigfield, A. (2012). Dimensions of reading motivation and their relation to reading behavior and competence. *Reading Research Quarterly, 47*(4), 427–463.

Schneider, M. (2002). *Do school facilities affect academic outcomes?* Washington, DC: National Clearinghouse for Educational Facilities.

Schneider, W. & Pressley, M. (1997). *Memory development between two and twenty, second edition*. Mahwah, NJ: Lawrence Erlbaum Associates.

Schnepf, S.V. (2007). Immigrants' educational disadvantage: An examination across ten countries and three surveys. *Journal of Population Economics, 20*(3), 527–545.

Sénéchal, M. & LeFevre, J.-A. (2002). Parental involvement in the development of children's reading skill: A five-year longitudinal study. *Child Development, 73*(2), 445–460.

Sénéchal, M. & Young, L. (2008). The effect of family interventions on children's acquisition of reading from Kindergarten to grade 3: A meta-analytic review. *Review of Educational Research, 78*(4), 880–907.

Shernoff, D.J., Csikszentmihalyi, M., Shneider, B., & Shernoff, E.S. (2003). Student engagement in high school classrooms from the perspective of flow theory. *School Psychology Quarterly, 18*(2), 158–176.

Sirin, S.R. (2005). Socioeconomic status and academic achievement: A meta-analytic review of research. *Review of Educational Research, 75*(3), 417–453.

Smith, M., Mikulecky, L. Kibby, M., & Dreher, M. (2000). What will be the demands of literacy in the workplace in the next millennium? *Reading Research Quarterly, 35*(3), 378–383.

Snow, C. (2002). *Reading for understanding: Toward an R&D program in reading comprehension.* Santa Monica, CA: RAND.

Sonnenschein, S. & Munsterman, K. (2002). The influence of home-based reading interactions on 5-year-olds' reading motivations and early literacy development. *Early Childhood Research Quarterly, 17*(3) 318–337.

Springer, L., Stanne, M.E., & Donovan, S.S. (1999). Effects of small-group learning on undergraduates in science, mathematics, engineering, and technology: A meta-analysis. *Review of Educational Research, 69*(21), 21–51.

Stanco, G. (2012). *Using TIMSS 2007 data to examine STEM school effectiveness in an international context* (Doctoral dissertation, Boston College). Retrieved from http://dcollections.bc.edu/webclient/StreamGate?folder_id=0&dvs=1383665793911~957

Stevenson, D.L. & Baker, D.P. (1992). Shadow education and allocation in formal schooling: Transition to university in Japan. *American Journal of Sociology, 97*(6), 1639–1657.

Stiggins, R. (1982). An analysis of the dimensions of job-related reading. *Reading World, 21*(3), 237–247.

Stone, C.L. (1983). A meta-analysis of advance organizer studies. *The Journal of Experimental Education, 51*(4), 194–199.

Stronge, J.H., Ward, T.J., & Grant, L.W. (2011). What makes good teachers good? A cross-case analysis of the connection between teacher effectiveness and student achievement. *Journal of Teacher Education, 62*(4), 339–355.

Taboada, A., Tonks, S., Wigfield, A., & Guthrie, J. (2009). Effects of motivational and cognitive variables on reading comprehension. *Reading and Writing: An Interdisciplinary Journal, 22*(1), 85–106.

Takeuchi, L.M. (2011). *Families matter: Designing media for a digital age.* New York: The Joan Ganz Cooney Center at Sesame Workshop.

Taras, H. (2005). Nutrition and student performance at school. *Journal of School Health, 75*(6), 199–213.

Taylor, B.M., Pearson, P.D., Clark, K., & Walpole, S. (2000). Effective schools and accomplished teachers: Lessons about primary-grade reading instruction in low-income schools. *The Elementary School Journal, 101*(2), 121–165.

Taylor, L.C., Clayton, J.D., & Rowley, S.J. (2004). Academic socialization: Understanding parental influences on children's school-related development in the early years. *Review of General Psychology, 8*(3), 163–178.

Therrien, W.J. (2004). Fluency and comprehension gains as a result of repeated reading: A meta-analysis. *Remedial and Special Education, 25*(4), 252–261.

Tillmann, L.C. (2005). Mentoring new teachers: Implications for leadership practice in an urban school. *Educational Administration Quarterly, 41*(4), 609–629.

Tokunaga, R.S. (2010). Following you home from school: A critical review and synthesis of research on cyberbullying victimization. *Computers in Human Behavior, 26*(3), 277–287.

Tondeur, J., van Braak, J., & Valcke, M. (2007). Towards a typology of computer use in primary education. *Journal of Computer Assisted Learning, 23*(3), 197–206.

Trautwein, U. (2007). The homework-achievement relation reconsidered: Differentiating homework time, homework frequency, and homework effort. *Learning and Instruction, 17*(3), 372–388.

Trong, K. (2009). *Using PIRLS 2006 to measure equity in reading achievement internationally* (Doctoral dissertation, Boston College). Retrieved from http://dcollections.bc.edu/webclient/StreamGate?folder_id=0&dvs=1383665979613~368

Tucker-Drob, E.M. (2012). Preschools reduce early academic-achievement gaps: A longitudinal twin approach. *Psychological Science, 23*(3), 310–319.

UNESCO Institute for Statistics. (2012). *International standard classification of education: ISCED 2011*. Montreal, Canada: United National Educational, Scientific and Cultural Organization (UNESCO). Retrieved from http://www.uis.unesco.org/Education/Documents/isced-2011-en.pdf

Van de Werfhorst, H.G. & Mijs, J.J.B. (2010). Achievement inequality and the institutional structures of educational systems: A comparative perspective. *Annual Review of Sociology, 36*(1), 407–428.

van Dijk, T. & Kintsch, W. (1983). *Strategies of discourse comprehension*. New York: Academic Press.

Vansteenkiste, M., Timmermans, T., Lens, W., Soenens, B., & Van den Broeck, A. (2008). Does extrinsic goal framing enhance extrinsic goal-oriented individuals' learning and performance? An experimental test of the match perspective versus self-determination theory. *Journal of Educational Psychology, 100*(2), 387–397.

Van Steensel, R., McElvany, N., Kurvers, J., & Herppich, S. (2011). How effective are family literacy programs? Results of a meta-analysis. *Review of Educational Research, 81*(1), 69–96.

Wang, M.C., Haertel, G.D., & Walberg, H.J. (1993). Toward a knowledge base for school learning. *Review of Educational Research, 63*(3), 249–294.

Weaver, C. & Kintsch, W. (1996). Expository text. In R. Barr, M.L. Kamil, P. Mosenthal, & P.D. Pearson (Eds.), *Handbook of reading research* (Vol. 2, pp. 230–245). Mahwah, NJ: Lawrence Erlbaum Associates.

West, R. & Stanovich, K. (2000). Automatic contextual facilitation in readers of three ages. In K. Stanovich (Ed.), *Progress in understanding reading* (pp. 13–20). New York: Guilford. (Adapted from (1978) Child Development, 49, 717–727.)

Wharton-McDonald, R. & Swiger, S. (2009). Developing higher order comprehension in the middle grades. In S. Israel & G. Duffy (Eds.), *Handbook of research on reading comprehension* (pp. 510–530). New York: Routledge.

Wheelan, S.A. & Kesselring, J. (2005). Link between faculty group development and elementary student performance on standardized tests. *The Journal of Educational Research, 98*(6), 323–330.

Willms, J.D. (2006). *Learning divides: Ten policy questions about the performance and equity of schools and schooling systems*. Montreal, Canada: UNESCO Institute for Statistics.

Witziers, B., Bosker, R.J., & Krüger, M.L. (2003). Educational leadership and student achievement: The elusive search for an association. *Educational Administration Quarterly, 39*(3), 398–425.

Wolf, R. (Ed.). (1995). *The IEA reading literacy study: Technical report*. The Hague, Netherlands: International Association for the Evaluation of Educational Achievement (IEA).

Wolfe, M. & Goldman, S. (2005). Relations between adolescents' text processing and reasoning. *Cognition and Instruction, 23*(4), 467–502.

Won, S.J. & Han, S. (2010). Out-of-school activities and achievement among middle school students in the US and South Korea. *Journal of Advanced Academics, 21*(4), 628–661.

Wright, S., Fugett, A., & Caputa, F. (2013). Using e-readers and Internet resources to support comprehension. *Educational Technology & Society, 16*(1), 367–379.

Wu, J.H., Hoy, W.K., & Tarter, C.J. (2013). Enabling school structure, collective responsibility, and a culture of academic optimism: Toward a robust model of school performance in Taiwan. *Journal of Educational Administration, 51*(2), 176–193.

Yair, G. (2000). Educational battlefields in America: The tug-of-war over students' engagement with instruction. *Sociology of Education, 73*(4), 247–269.

Yoon, K.S., Duncan, T., Lee, S.W.-Y., Scarloss, B., & Shapley, K.L. (2007). *Reviewing the evidence on how teacher professional development affects student achievement* (Institute of Education Sciences Report No. REL 2007-No.033). Washington, DC: US Department of Education.

Young, T.A. & Moss, B. (2006). Nonfiction in the classroom library: A literacy necessity. *Childhood Education, 82*(4), 207–212.

Zwaan, R. & Singer, M. (2003). Text comprehension. In A. Graesser, M. Gernsbacher, & S. Goldman (Eds.), *Handbook of discourse processes* (pp. 83–122). Mahwah, NJ: Lawrence Erlbaum Associates.

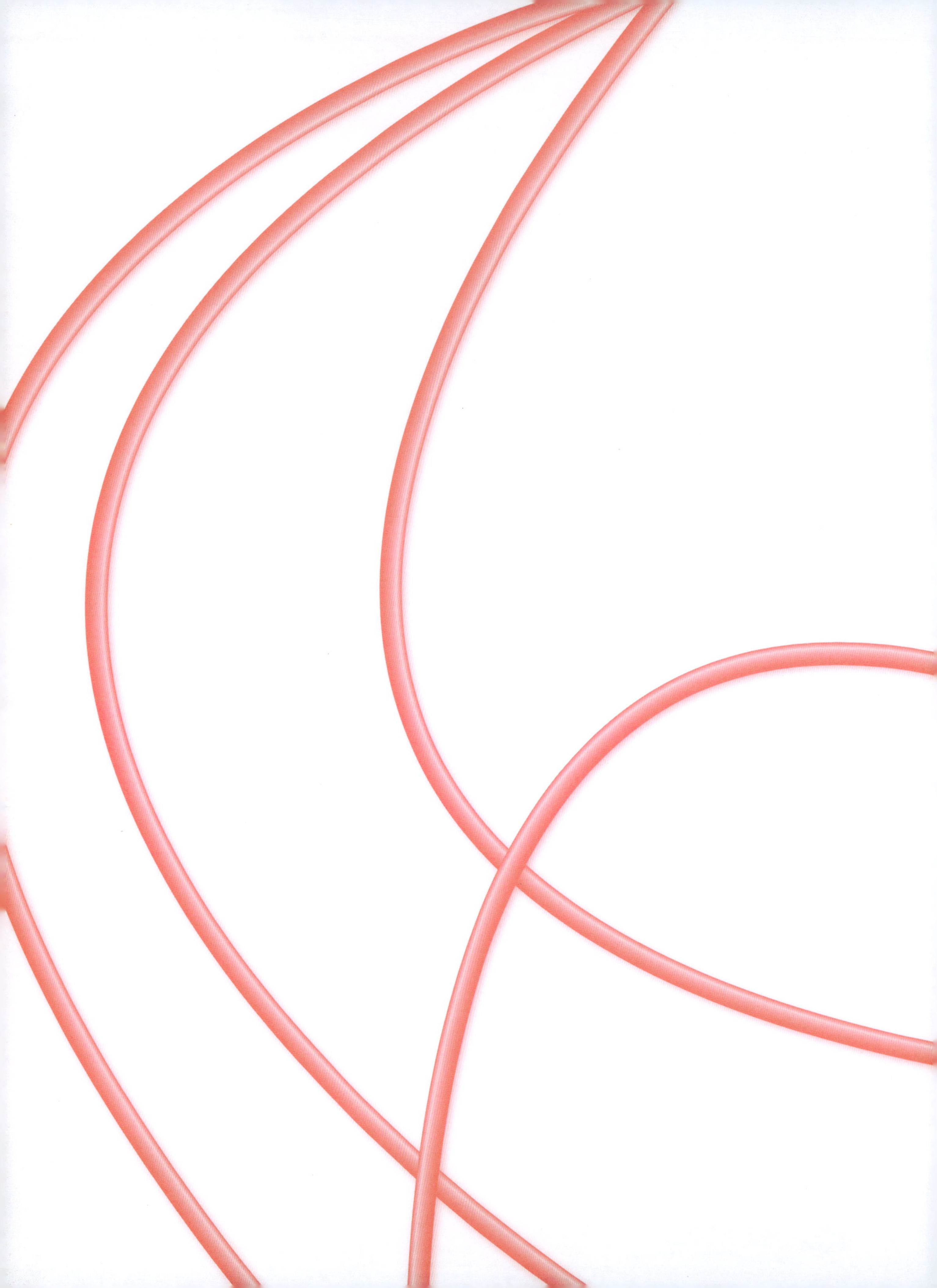

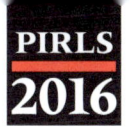

APPENDIX A

Acknowledgements

PIRLS is a major undertaking of IEA, and together with TIMSS (Trends in International Mathematics and Science Study), comprises the core of IEA's regular cycle of studies. IEA has delegated responsibility for the overall direction and management of these two projects to the TIMSS & PIRLS International Study Center at Boston College. Headed by Ina V.S. Mullis and Michael O. Martin, the study center is located in the Lynch School of Education. In carrying out these two ambitious international studies, the TIMSS & PIRLS International Study Center works closely with the IEA Secretariat in Amsterdam and the IEA Data Processing and Research Center in Hamburg. Statistics Canada monitors and implements sampling activities, the National Foundation for Educational Research (NFER) in England and the Australian Council for Educational Research (ACER) provide support for item development, and Educational Testing Service consults on psychometrics. Especially important is close coordination with the National Research Coordinators designated by the participating countries to be responsible for the complex tasks involved in implementing the studies in their countries. In summary, it takes extreme dedication on the part of many individuals around the world to make PIRLS a success and the work of these individuals across all of the various activities involved is greatly appreciated.

With each new assessment cycle of a study, one of the most important tasks is to update the assessment framework. Updating the PIRLS assessment framework for 2016 has involved extensive input and reviews by individuals at the TIMSS & PIRLS International Study, the IEA, the PIRLS 2016 National Research Coordinators, and the two PIRLS expert committees: the PIRLS 2016 Reading Development Group, and the PIRLS 2016 Questionnaire Development Group. Of all the individuals around the world that it takes to make PIRLS a success, the intention here is to specifically acknowledge some of those persons who had particular responsibility and involvement in developing and producing the *PIRLS 2016 Assessment Framework*.

PIRLS 2016 Framework Development at the TIMSS & PIRLS International Study Center at Boston College

Ina V.S. Mullis, Executive Director, TIMSS & PIRLS

Michael O. Martin, Executive Director, TIMSS & PIRLS

Pierre Foy, Director of Sampling, Psychometrics, and Data Analysis

Chad Minnich, Assistant Director, Communications & Media Relations

Martin Hooper, Senior Research Specialist, Technical Reporting

Marian Sainsbury, Chief Reading Consultant, National Foundation for Educational Research (NFER), England

PIRLS 2016 Reading Development Group

The PIRLS Reading Development Group is a panel of internationally recognized experts in reading research, instruction, and assessment. The Reading Development Group is responsible for providing expert advice about the development of the PIRLS 2016 reading assessment, beginning with updating the assessment framework and then test development for PIRLS, PIRLS Literacy, and ePIRLS.

Julian Fraillon
Australian Council for Educational Research
Australia

Jan Mejding
Aarhus University
Department of Education
Denmark

Galina Zuckerman
Russian Academy of Education
Russian Federation

Elizabeth Pang
Ministry of Education
Singapore

Jenny Wiksten Folkeryd
Uppsala University
Sweden

Ahlam Habeeb Msaiqer
Abu Dhabi Education Council
United Arab Emirates, Abu Dhabi

Donald Leu
University of Connecticut
United States

Karen Wixson
University of North Carolina, Greensboro
United States

PIRLS 2016 Questionnaire Development Group

The PIRLS 2016 Questionnaire Development Group comprises PIRLS 2016 National Research Coordinators who have special responsibility for providing guidance in updating the context questionnaire framework and context questionnaires for PIRLS 2016.

Joanne Latourelle
Ministère de l'Éducation, du Loisir et du Sport
Canada, Quebec

Hwa Wei Ko
National Central University
Chinese Taipei

Marc Colmant
Ministère de l'Éducation Nationale
France

Maryam A. Al-Ostad
National Centre for Education Development
Kuwait

Megan Chamberlain
Ministry of Education
New Zealand

Sarah Howie
University of Pretoria
South Africa

PIRLS 2016 National Research Coordinators

The PIRLS 2016 National Research Coordinators (NRCs) work with the PIRLS project staff in the various areas to ensure that the study is responsive to their concerns, both policy-oriented and practical, and are responsible for implementing the study in their countries. The PIRLS 2016 National Research Coordinators participated in a series of reviews of the *PIRLS 2016 Assessment Framework*.

Australia
Sue Thomson
Australian Council for Education Research

Austria
Birgit Suchán
Christina Wallner-Paschon
Bundesinstitut für Bildungsforchung, Innovation und Entwicklung des Österreichischen Schulwesens (BIFIE)

Azerbaijan
Narmina Aliyeva
Ministry of Education of the Republic of Azerbaijan

Bahrain
Huda Al-Awadi
Counselor for Research & Studies
Ministry of Education

Belgium (Flemish)
Kim Bellens
Centrum voor Onderwijseffectiviteit en evaluatie

Belgium (French)
Geneviève Hindryckx
Anne Matoul
Université de Liège

Botswana
Chawangwa Mudongo
Council of Ministers
Botswana Examinations Council

Bulgaria
Marina Vasileva Mavrodieva
Center for Control and Assessment of the Quality in Education
Ministry of Education, Youth and Science

Canada
Pierre Brochu
Council of Ministers of Education

Chile
Maria Victoria Martinez Muñoz
Estudios Internacionales Division de Estudios
Agencia de Calidad de la Educación

Chinese Taipei
Hwa Wei Ko
Graduate Institute of Learning and Instruction
National Central University

Czech Republic
Zuzana Janotová
Czech School Inspectorate

Denmark
Jan Mejding
Aarhus University
Department of Education

Egypt
Shokry Sayed Ahmed
National Center of Examinations and Educational Evaluation

England
Kath Thomas
Head of Assessment Design, Innovation and Standards

Finland
Inga Carita Arffman
Finnish Institute for Educational Research
University of Jyväskylä

France
Marc Colmant
Ministère de l'Éducation Nationale
Direction de l'Evaluation, de la Prospective et de la Performance

Georgia
Natia Andguladze
Nutsa Kobakhidze
National Assessment and Examinations Center

Germany
Wilfried Bos
Anke Walzebug
Center for School Development Research
University of Dortmund

Hong Kong SAR
Shek Kam Tse
Faculty of Education
University of Hong Kong

Hungary
Ildikó Balazsi
Péter Balkányi
Educational Authority
Department of Assessment and Evaluation

Iran, Islamic Republic of
Abdol'azim Karimi
Organization for Educational Research and Planning
National Center of TIMSS & PIRLS
Research Institute for Education

Ireland
Eemer Eivers
Educational Research Centre
St. Patrick's College, Dublin

Israel
Inbal Ron-Kaplan
National Authority for Measurement and Evaluation in Education (RAMA)
Ministry of Education

Italy
Laura Palmerio
Elisa Caponera (through 2013)
Istituto Nazionale per la Valutazione del Sistema Educativo di Istruzione e di Formazione (INVALSI)

Kazakhstan
Gulmira Berdibayeva
The National Centre for Assessment of the Quality of Education
Ministry of Education and Science of the Republic of Kazakhstan

Kuwait
Maryam A. Al-Ostad
National Centre for Education Development

Lithuania
Irina Mackevičienė
Ministry of Education and Science
National Examinations Center

Malta
Charles Mifsud
University of Malta
Grace Grima (through 2013)
Ministry of Education
Directorate for Quality and Standards in Education

Morocco
Mohammed Sassi
Ministère de l'Éducation Nationale
Centre Nationale de l'Evaluation et des Examens

Netherlands
Andrea Netten
Expertisecentrum Nederlands
National Language Education Center

New Zealand
Megan Chamberlain
Ministry of Education
Comparative Education Research Unit

Northern Ireland
Helen Irwin
Department of Education Statistics and Research Team

Norway
Egil Gabrielsen
National Center for Reading Education and Research
University of Stavanger

Oman
Zuwaina Saleh Al-Maskari
Ministry of Education

Poland
Michał Federowicz
Krzysztof Konarzewski
Educational Research Institute

Portugal
João Maroco
Instituto de Avaliacao Educativa, I.P.
Ana Sousa Ferreira (through 2013)
International Projects for Student Assessment
Ministry of Education and Science

Qatar
Saada Hassan Alobaidli
Supreme Education Council
Evaluation Institute

Russian Federation
Galina Kovaleva
Russian Academy of Education
Institute of Content and Methods of Education
Center for Evaluating the Quality of Secondary Education

Saudi Arabia
Mohammed Majre Al-Sobely
General Director of Evaluation
Ministry of Education

Singapore
Ng Huey Bian
Elizabeth Pang
Ministry of Education

Slovak Republic
Eva Ladányiová
Soňa Gallová (through 2013)
National Institute for Certified Educational Measurements (NUCEM)

Slovenia
Marjeta Doupona
Educational Research Institute

South Africa
Sarah Howie
Center for Evaluation and Assessment (CEA)
University of Pretoria

Spain
Jose Maria Sanchez-Echave
Instituto Nacional de Evaluación Educativa
Ministerio de Educación Cultura y Deporte

Sweden
Agnes Tongur
Tomas Matti
Swedish National Agency for Education

Trinidad and Tobago
Peter Smith
Ministry of Education
Division of Educational Research and Evaluation

United Arab Emirates
Nada Abu Baker Husain Ruban
Aljawhara Ali AlBakri Al Sebaiei
Ministry of Education
Assessment Department

United States
Sheila Thompson
National Center for Education Statistics
US Department of Education

Benchmarking Participants

Buenos Aires, Argentina
Silvia Montoya
Buenos Aires City Government
Ministry of Education

Ontario, Canada
Richard Jones
Education Quality and Accountability Office

Quèbec, Canada
Joanne Latourelle
Ministère de l'Éducation, du Loisir et du Sport Sanction des études

Spain (Andalusia)
Sebastian Cardenas Zabala
Agencia Andaluza de Evaluacion

United Arab Emirates (Abu Dhabi)
Shaikha Al Zaabi
Ahlam Habeeb Obaid Msaiger
Abu Dhabi Education Council
Assessment Department

United Arab Emirates (Dubai)
Mariam Al Ali
Rabaa AlSumaiti
Knowledge and Human Development Authority (KHDA)

A

PIRLS 2016 FRAMEWORK: ACKNOWLEDGEMENTS

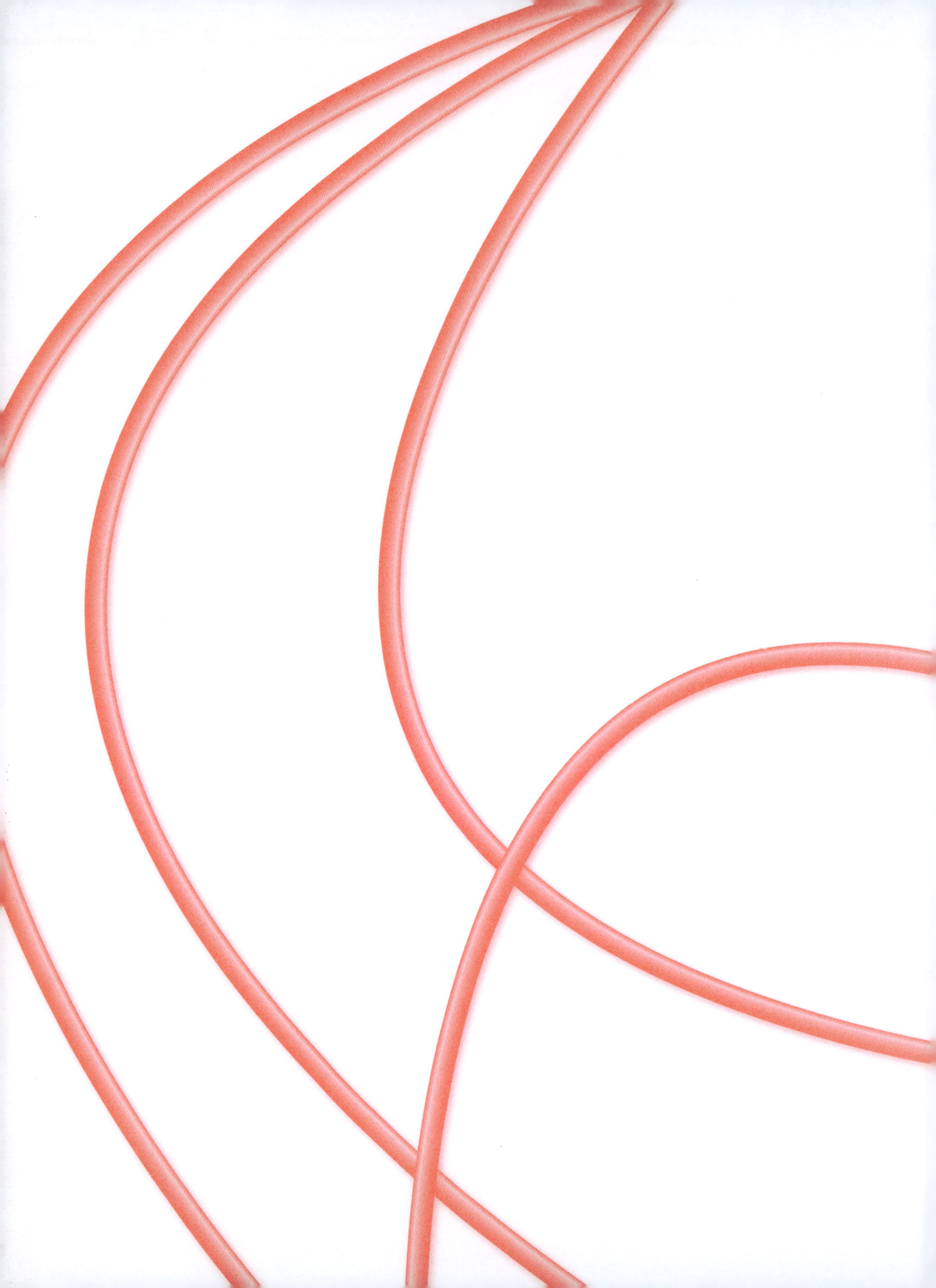

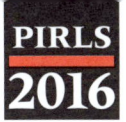

APPENDIX B

Sample PIRLS Passages, Questions, and Scoring Guides

Reading for Literary Experience

Enemy Pie

Reading to Acquire and Use Information

The Mystery of the Giant Tooth

Enemy Pie

by Derek Munson
illustrated by Tara Calahan King

It was a perfect summer until Jeremy Ross moved in right next door to my best friend Stanley. I did not like Jeremy. He had a party and I wasn't even invited. But my best friend Stanley was.

I never had an enemy until Jeremy moved into the neighborhood. Dad told me that when he was my age, he had enemies, too. But he knew of a way to get rid of them.

Dad pulled a worn-out scrap of paper from a recipe book.

"Enemy Pie," he said, satisfied.

You may be wondering what exactly is in Enemy Pie. Dad said the recipe was so secret, he couldn't even tell me. I begged him to tell me something—anything.

"I will tell you this, Tom," he said to me. "Enemy Pie is the fastest known way to get rid of enemies."

This got me thinking. What kinds of disgusting things would I put into Enemy Pie? I brought Dad earthworms and rocks, but he gave them right back.

I went outside to play. All the while, I listened to the sounds of my dad in the kitchen. This could be a great summer after all.

I tried to imagine how horrible Enemy Pie must smell. But I smelled something really good. As far as I could tell, it was coming from our kitchen. I was confused.

I went inside to ask Dad what was wrong. Enemy Pie shouldn't smell this good. But Dad was smart. "If it smelled bad, your enemy would never eat it," he said. I could tell he'd made this pie before.

The oven buzzer rang. Dad put on oven mitts and pulled out the pie. It looked good enough to eat! I was beginning to understand.

But still, I wasn't sure how this Enemy Pie worked. What exactly did it do to enemies? Maybe it made their hair fall out, or their breath stinky. I asked Dad, but he was no help.

While the pie cooled, Dad filled me in on my job.

He whispered. "In order for it to work, you need to spend a day with your enemy. Even worse, you have to be nice to him. It's not easy. But that's the only way that Enemy Pie can work. Are you sure you want to do this?"

Of course I was.

All I had to do was spend one day with Jeremy, then he'd be out of my life. I rode my bike to his house and knocked on the door.

When Jeremy opened the door, he seemed surprised.

"Can you come out and play?" I asked.

He looked confused. "I'll go ask my mom," he said. He came back with his shoes in his hand.

We rode bikes for awhile, then ate lunch. After lunch we went over to my house.

It was strange, but I was having fun with my enemy. I couldn't tell Dad that, since he had worked so hard to make the pie.

We played games until my dad called us for dinner.

Dad had made my favorite food. It was Jeremy's favorite, too! Maybe Jeremy wasn't so bad after all. I was beginning to think that maybe we should forget about Enemy Pie.

"Dad", I said, "It sure is nice having a new friend." I was trying to tell him that Jeremy was no longer my enemy. But Dad only smiled and nodded. I think he thought I was just pretending.

But after dinner, Dad brought out the pie. He dished up three plates and passed one to me and one to Jeremy.

"Wow!" Jeremy said, looking at the pie.

I panicked. I didn't want Jeremy to eat Enemy Pie! He was my friend!

"Don't eat it!" I cried. "It's bad!"

Jeremy's fork stopped before reaching his mouth. He looked at me funny. I felt relieved. I had saved his life.

"If it's so bad," Jeremy asked, "then why has your dad already eaten half of it?"

Sure enough, Dad was eating Enemy Pie.

"Good stuff," Dad mumbled. I sat there watching them eat. Neither one of them was losing any hair! It seemed safe, so I took a tiny taste. It was delicious!

After dessert, Jeremy invited me to come over to his house the next morning.

As for Enemy Pie, I still don't know how to make it. I still wonder if enemies really do hate it or if their hair falls out or their breath turns bad. But I don't know if I'll ever get an answer, because I just lost my best enemy.

Questions   Enemy Pie

1. Who is telling the story?

    Ⓐ Jeremy

    Ⓑ Dad

    Ⓒ Stanley

    Ⓓ Tom

2. At the beginning of the story, why did Tom think Jeremy was his enemy?

    _____
    _____

3. Write **one** ingredient that Tom thought would be in Enemy Pie.

    _____

4. Find the part of the story next to the picture of a piece of pie: . Why did Tom think it could be a great summer after all?

- Ⓐ He liked playing outside.
- Ⓑ He was excited about Dad's plan.
- Ⓒ He made a new friend.
- Ⓓ He wanted to taste Enemy Pie.

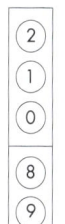

5. How did Tom feel when he first smelled Enemy Pie? Explain why he felt this way.

_____

_____

_____

6. What did Tom think could happen when his enemy ate Enemy Pie? Write **one** thing.

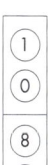

_____

_____

7. What were the **two** things Tom's dad told Tom to do for Enemy Pie to work?

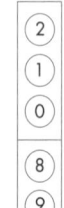

   _____

   _____

8. Why did Tom go to Jeremy's house?

   Ⓐ   To invite Jeremy to dinner.

   Ⓑ   To ask Jeremy to leave Stanley alone.

   Ⓒ   To invite Jeremy to play.

   Ⓓ   To ask Jeremy to be his friend.

9. What surprised Tom about the day he spent with Jeremy?

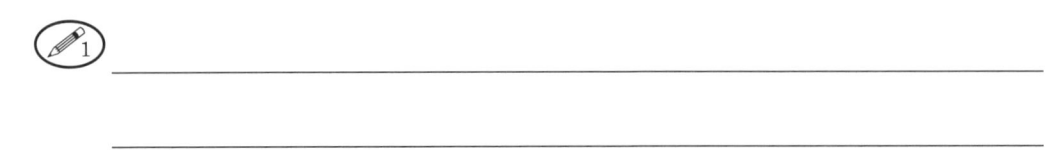

   _____

   _____

10. At dinner, why did Tom begin to think he and his dad should forget about Enemy Pie?

   Ⓐ Tom did not want to share dessert with Jeremy.

   Ⓑ Tom did not think Enemy Pie would work.

   Ⓒ Tom was beginning to like Jeremy.

   Ⓓ Tom wanted to keep Enemy Pie a secret.

11. How was Tom feeling when Dad passed the piece of Enemy Pie to Jeremy?

   Ⓐ alarmed

   Ⓑ satisfied

   Ⓒ surprised

   Ⓓ confused

12. What was it about Enemy Pie that Dad kept secret?

    Ⓐ It was a normal pie.

    Ⓑ It tasted disgusting.

    Ⓒ It was his favorite food.

    Ⓓ It was a poisonous pie.

13. Look at this sentence from the end of the story:

    "After dessert, Jeremy invited me to come over to his house the next morning."

    What does this suggest about the boys?

    Ⓐ They are still enemies.

    Ⓑ They do not like to play at Tom's house.

    Ⓒ They wanted to eat some more Enemy Pie.

    Ⓓ They might be friends in the future.

14. Use what you have read to explain why Tom's dad really made Enemy Pie.

    _____

    _____

    _____

15. What kind of person is Tom's dad? Give an example of what he did in the story that shows this.

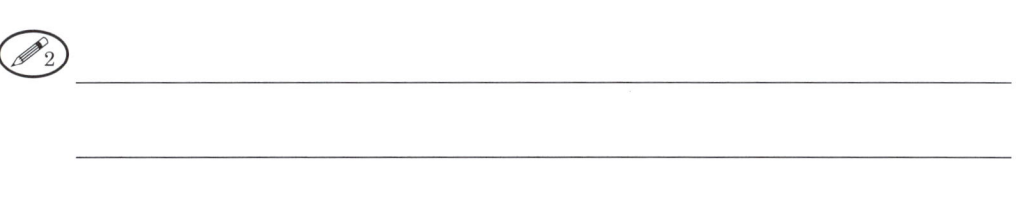

_____

_____

_____

16. What lesson might you learn from this story?

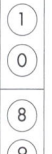

_____

_____

Scoring Guides for Constructed-response Questions

Enemy Pie, Item 2

2. At the beginning of the story, why did Tom think Jeremy was his enemy?

Purpose: Literary
Process: Make Straightforward Inferences

1 – Acceptable Response

The response shows understanding that Tom considered Jeremy his enemy, either because Jeremy did not invite him to his party, or because Jeremy invited Tom's best friend Stanley and not him.

Examples:

Tom was not invited to Jeremy's party.
Jeremy invited his friend to his party, but did not invite Tom.

OR, the response shows understanding that Tom was afraid that Jeremy would take his place as Stanley's best friend.

Examples:

Tom was jealous of him moving in next to Stanley.
Jeremy took his best friend.

0 – Unacceptable Response

The response does not show understanding of why Tom considered Jeremy his enemy. The response may repeat words from the question, or may provide a vague response that acknowledges that Jeremy moved in next door to Stanley or invited him to his party without showing understanding of the consequence.

Examples:

Jeremy was his enemy.
Jeremy moved in right next door to Tom's best friend.
Jeremy invited Stanley to his party.
Jeremy was new in the neighborhood.
Jeremy was his friend.

Non-Response Codes

8 – Not administered. Question misprinted, page missing, or other reason out of student's control.

9 – Blank

Enemy Pie, Item 3

3. Write one ingredient that Tom thought would be in Enemy Pie.

Purpose: Literary
Process: Focus on and Retrieve Explicitly Stated Information

1 – Acceptable Response

The response identifies either (earth)worms or rocks as an ingredient.

NOTE TO SCORERS: Do not credit responses that include ANY incorrect piece(s) of information alongside correct answers.

Answers:

earthworms

worms

rock

0 – Unacceptable Response

The response does not provide either of the ingredients listed above. The response may provide a vague description without mention of a specific ingredient, may name an incorrect ingredient alongside a correct response, or may describe what would happen to someone who ate the pie.

Examples:

rocks and dirt

worms and raspberries

disgusting things

secret ingredients

things that make your hair fall out

Non-Response Codes

8 – Not administered. Question misprinted, page missing, or other reason out of student's control.

9 – Blank

Enemy Pie, Item 5

5. How did Tom feel when he first smelled Enemy Pie? Explain why he felt this way.

Purpose: Literary
Process: Make Straightforward Inferences

2 – Complete Comprehension

The response shows understanding that Tom was confused because he thought Enemy Pie was supposed to smell bad, or that Tom was surprised because the pie his dad made (actually) smelled good.

NOTE TO SCORERS: Students may express Tom's confused or surprised feelings in a variety of ways.

Examples:

confused because he thought it was made with disgusting things

He didn't understand. It should taste horrible.

He felt unsure. Enemy Pie should smell bad.

surprised because it smelled really good

1 – Partial Comprehension

The response shows understanding that Tom was confused or surprised when he smelled Enemy Pie for the first time, but does not explain why.

Examples:

confused

He wondered what was going on.

OR, the response explains that Enemy Pie didn't smell the way he thought it would without providing the feeling.

Examples:

Enemy Pie shouldn't smell this good.

He thought the pie would smell bad.

He thought it would smell awful, but it didn't.

0 – No Comprehension

The response does not provide either the appropriate feeling or an explanation.

Examples:

He smelled something really good. *(Please note that this response does not provide a feeling or a clear explanation for why Tom was confused.)*

He felt hungry.

Non-Response Codes

8 – Not administered. Question misprinted, page missing, or other reason out of student's control.

9 – Blank

Enemy Pie, Item 6

6. What did Tom think could happen when his enemy ate Enemy Pie? Write one thing.

Purpose: Literary
Process: Focus on and Retrieve Explicitly Stated Information

1 – Acceptable Response

The response identifies one of the consequences of eating Enemy Pie from the list below.

NOTE TO SCORERS: Ignore minor variations in phrasing from the text, as long as it is clear what is intended.

Consequences of Eating Enemy Pie:

His hair would fall out.

His breath would stink.

He would go away.

Something bad would happen./He would get sick (or die).

0 – Unacceptable Response

The response does not provide any of the words or phrases in the list above. The response may repeat words from the question.

Examples:

He might like it.

He would become his friend.

Nothing would happen.

He would become his enemy.

Non-Response Codes

8 – Not administered. Question misprinted, page missing, or other reason out of student's control.

9 – Blank

Enemy Pie, Item 7

7. What were the two things Tom's dad told Tom to do for Enemy Pie to work?

Purpose: Literary
Process: Focus on and Retrieve Explicitly Stated Information

2 – Complete Comprehension

The response identifies both actions that make Enemy Pie work: 1) spending the day with his enemy, and 2) being nice to him.

NOTE TO SCORERS: Any responses that do not include specific reference to the amount of time that should be spent (a day) should not be credited.

Examples:

be nice to his enemy for a whole day

spend the whole day with Jeremy and be nice

be nice and play with him for a day

play all day with Jeremy and be friendly

1 – Partial Comprehension

The response provides one action that Tom was told to do by his Dad.

Examples:

be nice

spend the day with him

play and be nice

0 – No Comprehension

The response does not provide an accurate action that Tom was told to do by his Dad.

Examples:

play with him *(Please note that this is not one of the things Tom's dad told him to do and is too vague to be considered as a paraphrase of either spending the day or being nice.)*

stop being enemies *(Please note that Tom's dad did not tell him to stop being enemies with Jeremy, nor did he tell him to be his friend.)*

invite him over for dinner

eat Enemy Pie

Non-Response Codes

8 – Not administered. Question misprinted, page missing, or other reason out of student's control.

9 – Blank

Enemy Pie, Item 9

9. What surprised Tom about the day he spent with Jeremy?

Purpose: Literary
Process: Make Straightforward Inferences

1– Acceptable Response

The response shows understanding that Tom had a positive experience with Jeremy. The response may indicate that he enjoyed spending time with Jeremy, that Jeremy wasn't as bad as Tom expected, or that they had become friends.

Examples:

He was actually having fun with Jeremy.

They were getting along.

Jeremy wasn't so bad after all.

Jeremy was nice.

They became friends.

It was a good day.

0 – Unacceptable Response

The response does not accurately describe what surprised Tom.

Examples:

Tom was surprised.

Jeremy was going to eat the Enemy Pie.

Non-Response Codes

8 – Not administered. Question misprinted, page missing, or other reason out of student's control.

9 – Blank

Enemy Pie, Item 14

14. Use what you have read to explain why Tom's dad really made Enemy Pie.

Purpose: Literary
Process: Interpret and Integrate Ideas and Information

1- Acceptable Response

The response demonstrates understanding that Tom's dad's plan for Enemy Pie was for Tom and Jeremy to become friends.

> NOTE TO SCORERS: The response does not need to explicitly state that Tom's dad made them spend time together to be awarded credit.

> Examples:

to make them be friends and not enemies

He wanted them to be friends.

to get them to play together and to make them friends

He wanted them to be friends so he got them to play with each other.

to play a trick for Tom to see that Jeremy was nice after all *(Please note that this is an acceptable paraphrase of the boys becoming friends.)*

0 – Unacceptable Response

The response does not provide an appropriate explanation for why Tom's dad really made Enemy Pie. The response may indicate that Tom's dad wanted the boys to spend time together without specific reference to the intended outcome, or it may refer generally to Tom having no enemies without reference to Tom and Jeremy's relationship.

> Examples:

He made Tom play with Jeremy.

So they would get to know each other.

He thought it would work and make Jeremy leave.

He made the pie for them all to share.

Non-Response Codes

8 – Not administered. Question misprinted, page missing, or other reason out of student's control.

9 – Blank

Enemy Pie, Item 15

15. What kind of person is Tom's dad? Give an example of what he did in the story that shows this.

Purpose: Literary
Process: Interpret and Integrate Ideas and Information

2 – Complete Comprehension

The response describes one plausible character trait of Tom's dad that is central to his role in the story (e.g., helpful, caring, nice, good, smart, clever, tricky, secretive). In addition, the response provides one example of Tom's dad's actions that is evidence of the character trait.

NOTE TO SCORERS: Traits may be expressed as a longer description, rather than as a single word.

Examples:

He was caring because he wanted to help his son make friends.

He was smart in how he found a way for the boys to like each other.

He was the kind of person who kept secrets. He kept Tom from finding out that Enemy Pie was just a normal pie.

He was nice. He wanted Tom and Jeremy to get along.

Tom's dad was kind. He thought of a plan for his son to make friends.

1 – Partial Comprehension

The response provides one plausible character trait of Tom's dad that is central to his role in the story (e.g., helpful, caring, smart, clever, tricky, secretive). Traits may be expressed as a longer description, rather than as a single word.

Examples:

He was caring.

He was nice.

He was a good person.

He was a good dad.

He cared about his son.

He wanted to help Tom.

He was clever. He made a pie. *(Please note that "he made a pie" is not an appropriate example of Tom's dad's cleverness.)*

0 – No Comprehension

The response does not provide an appropriate description of Tom's dad's character. The response may provide a general character trait of Tom's dad that is not supported by the text, or a vague description that demonstrates limited comprehension of the story without further textual support.

Examples:

Tom's dad was mean.

He was confused. *(Please note that this response describes Tom in the story.)*

He was a cook. He baked a pie. *(Please note that "he was a cook" is not a character description.)*

OR, the response may provide an example of Tom's dad's actions without providing a character trait.

Examples:

He made Tom think Enemy Pie would work.

He kept the recipe a secret.

He told Tom to play with Jeremy.

Non-Response Codes

8 – Not administered. Question misprinted, page missing, or other reason out of student's control.

9 – Blank

Enemy Pie, Item 16

16. What lesson might you learn from this story?

Purpose: Literary
Process: Examine and Evaluate Content, Language, and Textual Elements

1– Acceptable Response

The response provides an evaluation of the main message or theme of the story that acknowledges the importance of giving a relationship the chance to grow before deciding whether someone is your friend, or indicates that it is possible to change how you feel about someone.

Examples:

Don't judge someone before you know them.

You can make friends if you give it a chance.

Your enemy can become your friend.

Try to like your enemy. They might become your friend.

0 – Unacceptable Response

The response does not provide a plausible evaluation of the main message or theme of the story. The response may provide a main message that is too general, or may refer to a message that is not central to the story.

Examples:

Be nice to everyone.

You shouldn't have enemies. *(Please note that this is an inaccurate generalization of the main message.)*

Don't eat Enemy Pie.

It isn't nice to exclude someone from your party.

Non-Response Codes

8 – Not administered. Question misprinted, page missing, or other reason out of student's control.

9 – Blank

The GIANT Tooth Mystery

A fossil is the remains of any creature or plant that lived on the Earth many, many years ago. People have been finding fossils for thousands of years in rocks and cliffs and beside lakes. We now know that some of these fossils were from dinosaurs.

   Long ago, people who found huge fossils did not know what they were. Some thought the big bones came from large animals that they had seen or read about, such as hippos or elephants. But some of the bones people found were too big to have come from even the biggest hippo or elephant. These enormous bones led some people to believe in giants.

Hundreds of years ago in France, a man named Bernard Palissy had another idea. He was a famous pottery maker. When he went to make his pots, he found many tiny fossils in the clay. He studied the fossils and wrote that they were the remains of living creatures. This was not a new idea. But Bernard Palissy also wrote that some of these creatures no longer lived on earth. They had completely disappeared. They were extinct.

Was Bernard Palissy rewarded for his discovery? No! He was put in prison for his ideas.

As time went by, some people became more open to new ideas about how the world might have been long ago.

Then, in the 1820s, a huge fossil tooth was found in England. It is thought that Mary Ann Mantell, the wife of fossil expert Gideon Mantell was out for a walk when she saw what looked like a huge stone tooth. Mary Ann Mantell knew the big tooth was a fossil, and took it home to her husband.

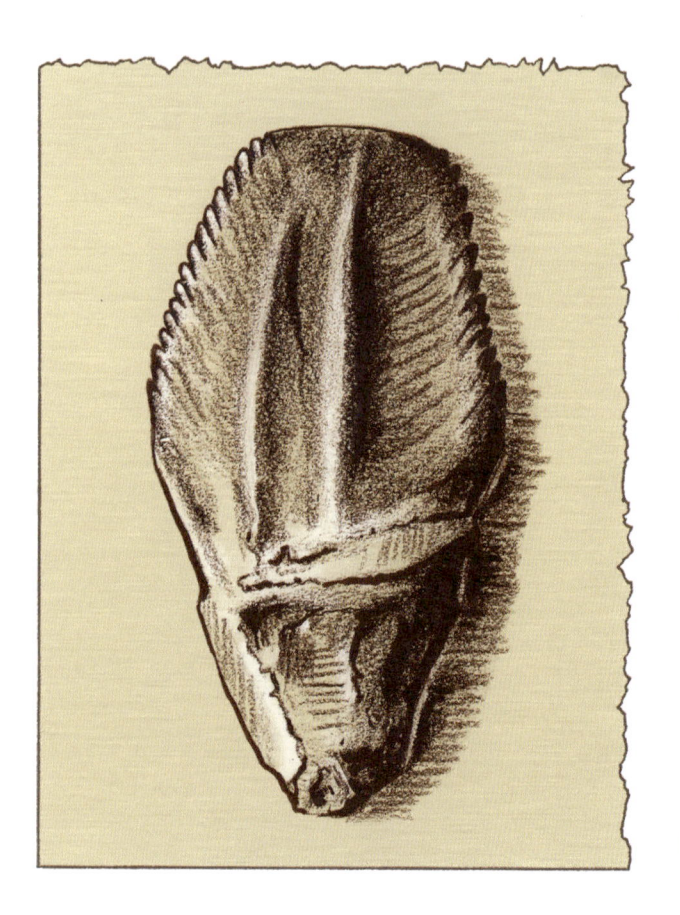

When Gideon Mantell first looked at the fossil tooth, he thought it had belonged to a plant eater because it was flat and had ridges. It was worn down from chewing food. It was almost as big as the tooth of an elephant. But it looked nothing like an elephant's tooth.

Fossil tooth sketched life-sized

Gideon Mantell could tell that the pieces of rock attached to the tooth were very old. He knew that it was the kind of rock where reptile fossils were found. Could the tooth have belonged to a giant, plant-eating reptile that chewed its food? A type of reptile that no longer lived on earth?

Gideon Mantell was really puzzled by the big tooth. No reptile that he knew about chewed its food. Reptiles gulped their food, and so their teeth didn't become worn down. It was a mystery.

Gideon Mantell took the tooth to a museum in London and showed it to other scientists. No one agreed with Gideon Mantell that it might be the tooth of a gigantic reptile.

Gideon Mantell tried to find a reptile that had a tooth that looked like the giant tooth. For a long time, he found nothing. Then one day he met a scientist who was studying iguanas. An iguana is a large plant-eating reptile found in Central and South America. It can grow to be more than five feet long. The scientist showed Gideon Mantell an iguana tooth. At last! Here was the tooth of a living reptile that looked like the mystery tooth. Only the fossil tooth was much, much bigger.

Iguana

A life-sized drawing of an iguana's tooth from Gideon Mantell's notebook

Now Gideon Mantell believed the fossil tooth had belonged to an animal that looked like an iguana. Only it wasn't five feet long. Gideon Mantell believed it was a hundred feet long! He named his creature *Iguanodon*. That means "iguana tooth".

Gideon Mantell did not have a whole *Iguanodon* skeleton. But from the bones he had collected over the years, he tried to figure out what one might have looked like. He thought the bones showed that the creature had walked on all four legs. He thought a pointed bone was a horn. He drew an *Iguanodon* with a horn on its nose.

What Gideon Mantell thought an Iguanodon looked like

Years later, several complete *Iguanodon* skeletons were found. They were only about thirty feet long. The bones showed that it walked on its hind legs some of the time. And what Gideon Mantell thought was a horn on its nose was really a spike on its "thumb"! Based on these discoveries, scientists changed their ideas about what the *Iguanodon* looked like.

Gideon Mantell made some mistakes. But he had made an important discovery, too. Since his first idea that the fossil tooth belonged to a plant-eating reptile, he spent many years gathering facts and evidence to prove his ideas were right. By making careful guesses along the way, Gideon Mantell was one of the first people to show that long ago, giant reptiles lived on earth. And then they became extinct.

Hundreds of years before, Bernard Palissy had been thrown in prison for saying nearly the same thing. But Gideon Mantell became famous. His discovery made people curious to find out more about these huge reptiles.

What scientists today think the Iguanodon looked like

In 1842, a scientist named Richard Owen decided that these extinct reptiles needed a name of their own. He called them *Dinosauria*. This means "fearfully great lizard". Today we call them dinosaurs.

Questions   The Giant Tooth Mystery

1. What is a fossil?

    Ⓐ the surface of rocks and cliffs

    Ⓑ the bones of a giant

    Ⓒ the remains of very old living things

    Ⓓ the teeth of elephants

2. According to the article, why did some people long ago believe in giants?

    _____
    _____
    _____

3. Where did Bernard Palissy find fossils?

    Ⓐ on the cliffs

    Ⓑ in the clay

    Ⓒ by a river

    Ⓓ on a path

4. What was Bernard Palissy's new idea?

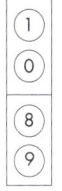

   ✏️ _____

5. Why was Bernard Palissy put into prison?

   Ⓐ People were not open to new ideas.

   Ⓑ He copied his ideas from Gideon Mantell.

   Ⓒ He left tiny fossils in his pottery.

   Ⓓ Studying fossils was forbidden in France.

6. Who found the fossil tooth in England?

   Ⓐ Bernard Palissy

   Ⓑ Mary Ann Mantell

   Ⓒ Richard Owen

   Ⓓ Gideon Mantell

7. What did Gideon Mantell know about reptiles that made the fossil tooth puzzling?

- Ⓐ Reptiles had no teeth.
- Ⓑ Reptiles were found under rocks.
- Ⓒ Reptiles lived long ago.
- Ⓓ Reptiles gulped their food.

8. Gideon Mantell thought the tooth might have belonged to different types of animals. Complete the table to show what made him think this.

Type of animal	What made him think this
A plant eater	The tooth was flat with ridges.
A giant creature	
A reptile	

9. Why did Gideon Mantell take the tooth to a museum?

- Ⓐ to ask if the fossil belonged to the museum
- Ⓑ to prove that he was a fossil expert
- Ⓒ to hear what scientists thought of his idea
- Ⓓ to compare the tooth with others in the museum

10. A scientist showed Gideon Mantell an iguana tooth. Why was this important to Gideon Mantell?

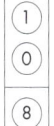

_____

_____

11. What did Gideon Mantell use when trying to figure out what the *Iguanodon* looked like?

- Ⓐ bones he collected
- Ⓑ ideas from other scientists
- Ⓒ pictures in books
- Ⓓ teeth from other reptiles

12. Look at the two pictures of the *Iguanodon*. What do they help you to understand?

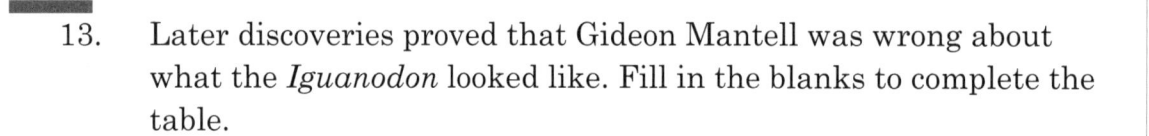

_____

_____

_____

13. Later discoveries proved that Gideon Mantell was wrong about what the *Iguanodon* looked like. Fill in the blanks to complete the table.

What Gideon Mantell thought the *Iguanodon* looked like	What scientists today think the *Iguanodon* looked like
The *Iguanodon* walked on four legs.	
	The *Iguanodon* had a spike on its thumb.
The *Iguanodon* was 100 feet long.	

14. What were found that showed Gideon was wrong about what the *Iguanodon* looked like?

   Ⓐ more fossil teeth

   Ⓑ scientific drawings

   Ⓒ living *Iguanodons*

   Ⓓ whole skeletons

Giant Tooth Mystery, Item 2

2. According to the article, why did some people long ago believe in giants?

Purpose: Acquire and Use Information
Process: Make Straightforward Inferences

1 – Acceptable Response

The response demonstrates understanding that people long ago believed in giants because they found huge bones/skeletons/fossils.

NOTE TO SCORERS: Some students use the word "giant" as a synonym for "big" or "huge". Such responses should be credited only where the meaning is made clear.

Examples:

They found bones too big to belong to something they knew.

They found giant bones that were too big to be from the biggest hippo.

They found really big bones.

The bones were so big they must be from giants.

0 – Unacceptable Response

The response does not demonstrate understanding that people long ago believe in giants because they found huge bones/skeletons/fossils.

Examples:

Giants are really big.

They found giant bones. *(Please note that the use of "giant" is ambiguous.)*

They found things that must belong to giants.

They found dinosaur bones.

They found bones from giants.

Non-Response Codes

8 – Not administered. Question misprinted, page missing, or other reason out of student's control.

9 – Blank

Giant Tooth Mystery, Item 4

4. What was Bernard Palissy's new idea?

Purpose: Acquire and Use Information
Process: Interpret and Integrate Ideas and Information

1 – Acceptable Response

The response demonstrates understanding that Palissy's new idea was that some fossils belonged to animals that no longer lived on earth, had completely disappeared, or were extinct.

Examples:

Fossils could be from extinct animals.

Some belonged to creatures no longer living on earth.

His idea was that some animals had completely disappeared!

0 – Unacceptable Response

The response does not demonstrate understanding of Palissy's new idea. It might relate to Palissy's idea that fossils once belonged to living creatures, or may state a fact about Palissy's work.

Examples:

Fossils were from the remains of living creatures.

Reptiles were extinct.

He found fossils in his clay.

He was a famous pottery maker.

He studied fossils.

Non-Response Codes

8 – Not administered. Question misprinted, page missing, or other reason out of student's control.

9 – Blank

Giant Tooth Mystery, Item 8

8. Gideon Mantell thought the tooth might have belonged to different types of animals. Complete the table to show what made him think this.

Type of animal	What made him think this
A plant eater	The tooth was flat with ridges
A giant creature	
A reptile	

Purpose: Acquire and Use Information
Process: Interpret and Integrate Ideas and Information

NOTE TO SCORERS: Each of the two parts of this item will be scored separately in its own 1-point coding block.

The entire item, with acceptable responses for each of the two parts and the corresponding coding blocks, should look like this:

Type of animal	What made him think this
A plant eater	The tooth was flat with ridges
A giant creature	The response identifies the large size of the fossil tooth (as big as an elephant's tooth)
A reptile	The response indicates that: 1) the rock in which it was found was the kind of rock where reptile fossils were found/it was found where reptiles had lived, OR 2) the fossil tooth was similar to/looked like an iguana/reptile tooth

A GIANT CREATURE

1 – Acceptable Response

The response shows understanding of the characteristics that indicate the fossil tooth could belong to a giant creature.

Type of animal	What made him think this
A plant eater	The tooth was flat with ridges
A giant creature	The response identifies the large size of the fossil tooth (as big as an elephant's tooth)
A reptile	The response indicates that: 1) the rock in which it was found was the kind of rock where reptile fossils were found/it was found where reptiles had lived, OR 2) the fossil tooth was similar to/looked like an iguana/reptile tooth

0 – Unacceptable Response

The response does not show understanding of the characteristics that indicate the fossil tooth could belong to a giant creature. The response may refer to the text at the beginning of the passage about fossils in general, rather than to Gideon's hypotheses about the fossil tooth.

Examples:

Some thought the big bones came from large animals.

It was worn down.

It looked like an elephant's tooth. *(Please note that this is an inaccurate response. The text states, "it looked nothing like an elephant's tooth.")*

Non-Response Codes

8 – Not administered. Question misprinted, page missing, or other reason out of student's control.

9 – Blank

A REPTILE

1 – Acceptable Response

The response shows understanding of the characteristics that indicate the fossil tooth could belong to a reptile.

Type of animal	What made him think this
A plant eater	The tooth was flat with ridges
A giant creature	The response identifies the large size of the fossil tooth (as big as an elephant's tooth)
A reptile	The response indicates that: 1) the rock in which it was found was the kind of rock where reptile fossils were found/it was found where reptiles had lived, OR 2) the fossil tooth was similar to/looked like an iguana/reptile tooth

0 – Unacceptable Response

The response does not show understanding of the characteristics that indicate the fossil tooth could belong to a reptile.

Examples:

It eats plants.

Reptiles gulped their food.

Non-Response Codes

8 – Not administered. Question misprinted, page missing, or other reason out of student's control.

9 – Blank

Giant Tooth Mystery, Item 10

10. A scientist showed Gideon Mantell an iguana tooth. Why was this important to Gideon Mantell?

Purpose: Acquire and Use Information
Process: Interpret and Integrate Ideas and Information

1 – Acceptable Response

The response demonstrates understanding that the iguana tooth provided evidence that supported Gideon Mantell's theory that the fossil tooth might have belonged to a giant reptile.

Examples:

The iguana tooth showed his fossil could be from a reptile.

It helped him find out what type of animal the tooth belonged to.

The tooth proved he was right.

It gave him proof for what he thought all along.

OR, the response demonstrates a more general understanding that the iguana tooth looked like the fossil tooth.

Examples:

The iguana tooth looked like the fossil tooth.

He could see that they looked the same.

He could tell it was the same one.

He had spent years looking for a matching tooth.

It was flat and had ridges.

0 – Unacceptable Response

The response does not demonstrate understanding of the significance of the iguana tooth.

Examples:

He wanted to be famous.

He thought it would be interesting to see an iguana's tooth.

He wanted to learn more about reptiles.

It showed he was clever. *(Please note that this response is too vague because it focuses on his personal characteristics rather than on his discovery.)*

He wanted to compare the teeth. *(Please note that this response fails to indicate the significance of the comparison.)*

Non-Response Codes

8 – Not administered. Question misprinted, page missing, or other reason out of student's control.

9 – Blank

Giant Tooth Mystery, Item 12

12. Look at the two pictures of the Iguanodon. What do they help you to understand?

Purpose: Acquire and Use Information
Process: Examine and Evaluate Content, Language, and Textual Elements

2 – Complete Comprehension

The response demonstrates understanding that the pictures show the changes in scientific ideas, or that the pictures show different people's ideas about the Iguanodon.

Examples:

that scientists today think the Iguanodon looked different than Gideon Mantell did

To show how people's ideas about what the Iguanodon looked like changed.

To show that different people had different ideas about what it looked like.

how different the ideas were

Gideon Mantell thought the bones showed the Iguanodon walked on all four legs, but later scientists changed their minds.

OR, the response indicates that the pictures illustrate the mistakes that Gideon Mantell or other people might have made.

Examples:

To show that Gideon got some things wrong.

that people sometimes make mistakes

1 – Partial Comprehension

The response demonstrates a more general understanding that the Iguanodons looked different in the two pictures.

Example:

To show they look different.

OR, the response describes a difference between the two pictures without reference to changes in scientific ideas or what different people might have believed.

Example:

One has 4 legs, the other has 2.

OR, the response provides an explicit reference to one of the pictures without reference to changes in scientific ideas or what different people might have believed.

Example:

That Gideon thought it had a horn.

0 – No Comprehension

The response does not demonstrate understanding of the purpose of the illustrations. The response may describe a specific feature from one of the pictures, or give a description of what the illustrations have in common.

OR, the response may provide an inaccurate interpretation that the Iguanodon itself changed in appearance over time, rather than people's ideas.

Examples:

To show what they looked like.

They help you understand how the Iguanodon changed over the years.

They show me they ate plants.

They had 4 legs.

Non-Response Codes

8 – Not administered. Question misprinted, page missing, or other reason out of student's control.

9 – Blank

Giant Tooth Mystery, Item 13

13. Later discoveries proved that Gideon Mantell was wrong about what the Iguanodon looked like. Fill in the blanks to complete the table.

What Gideon Mantell thought the Iguanodon looked like	What scientists today think the Iguanodon looked like
The Iguanodon walked on four legs	
	The Iguanodon had a spike on its thumb
The Iguanodon was 100 feet long	

Purpose: Acquire and Use Information
Process: Interpret and Integrate Ideas and Information

NOTE TO SCORERS: Each of the three parts of this item will be scored separately in its own 1-point coding block.

The entire item, with acceptable responses for each of the three parts and the corresponding coding blocks, should look like this:

What Gideon Mantell thought the Iguanodon looked like	What scientists today think the Iguanodon looked like	
The Iguanodon walked on four legs	The Iguanodon (sometimes) walked/ stood on two/hind legs	→ 1 0 8 9
The Iguanodon had a horn (on its head/face/nose) OR, the spike was on its head/face/nose	**The Iguanodon had a spike on its thumb**	→ 1 0 8 9
The Iguanodon was 100 feet long	The Iguanodon was 30 feet (9 metres) long	→ 1 0 8 9

1 – Acceptable Response

The response shows understanding of the difference in the way that Gideon Mantell and scientists today think the Iguanodon walked or stood.

What Gideon Mantell thought the Iguanodon looked like	What scientists today think the Iguanodon looked like
The Iguanodon walked on four legs	The Iguanodon (sometimes) walked/stood on two/hind legs
The Iguanodon had a horn (on its head/face/nose) OR, the spike was on its head/face/nose	The Iguanodon had a spike on its thumb
The Iguanodon was 100 feet long	The Iguanodon was 30 feet (9 metres) long

0 – Unacceptable Response

The response does not show understanding of the way scientists today think the Iguanodon walked or stood.

Examples:

two

It stood.

Non-Response Codes

8 – Not administered. Question misprinted, page missing, or other reason out of student's control.

9 – Blank

1 – Acceptable Response

The response shows understanding of the difference in where Gideon Mantell and scientists today think the Iguanodon had a spike.

What Gideon Mantell thought the Iguanodon looked like	What scientists today think the Iguanodon looked like
The Iguanodon walked on four legs	The Iguanodon (sometimes) walked/stood on two/hind legs
The Iguanodon had a horn (on its head/face/nose) OR, the spike was on its head/face/nose	The Iguanodon had a spike on its thumb
The Iguanodon was 100 feet long	The Iguanodon was 30 feet (9 metres) long

0 – Unacceptable Response

The response does not show understanding of where Gideon Mantell thought the Iguanodon had a spike.

Examples:

horn on its thumb

spike on its back

did not have a spike on its thumb

Non-Response Codes

8 – Not administered. Question misprinted, page missing, or other reason out of student's control.

9 – Blank

1 – Acceptable Response

The response shows understanding of the difference in what Mantell and scientists today think was the length of the Iguanodon.

What Gideon Mantell thought the Iguanodon looked like	What scientists today think the Iguanodon looked like
The Iguanodon walked on four legs	The Iguanodon (sometimes) walked/stood on two/hind legs
The Iguanodon had a horn (on its head/face/nose) OR, the spike was on its head/face/nose	**The Iguanodon had a spike on its thumb**
The Iguanodon was 100 feet long	The Iguanodon was 30 feet (9 metres) long

0 – Unacceptable Response

The response does not show understanding of how long scientists today think the Iguanodon was.

Examples:

It was not 100 feet long.

5 feet long

Non-Response Codes

8 – Not administered. Question misprinted, page missing, or other reason out of student's control.

9 – Blank

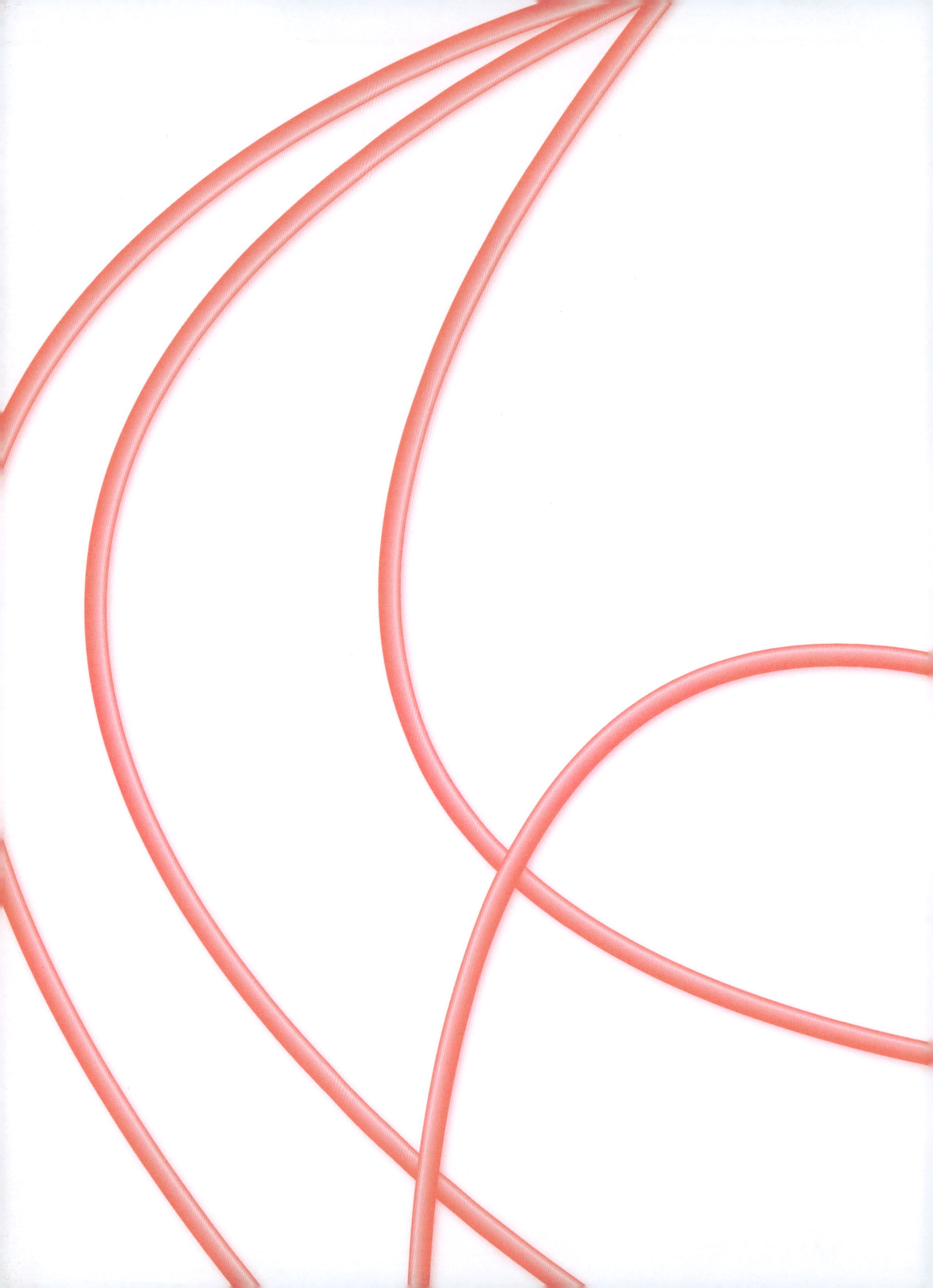

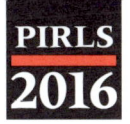

APPENDIX C

Sample PIRLS Literacy Passages, Questions, and Scoring Guides

Reading for Literary Experience

Brave Charlotte

Reading to Acquire and Use Information

Caterpillar to Butterfly

Brave Charlotte

By Anu Stohner
Illustrated by Henrike Wilson

Charlotte was different from all the other sheep right from the start. When all the other lambs just stood shyly by their mothers, Charlotte was leaping around, ready for adventure.

Charlotte lived with all the other sheep on a hillside far from the farm. They had a shepherd to look after them and he had an old dog named Jack. Jack tried to keep Charlotte under control, but she wasn't scared of him.

1. Who is Jack?

   _____

2. What did Jack try to do with Charlotte?

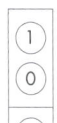

   _____

One time, Charlotte jumped over the side of a riverbank and went for a swim in the fast-running stream.

"Tut, tut," said the older sheep, shaking their heads.

What would they say if they knew that at night Charlotte secretly roamed through the countryside?

When all the other sheep were sleeping, she would slip away to her special place and gaze at the moon. Even Jack didn't notice. But he didn't have very good ears these days.

3. Give **two** ways that Charlotte was different from the other sheep.

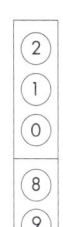

   1. _____
   _____

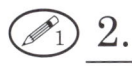

   2. _____
   _____

4. Where was Charlotte standing in the picture on the opposite page?

   - Ⓐ in her special place
   - Ⓑ by the stream
   - Ⓒ at the farm
   - Ⓓ in her hiding place

5. Why didn't Jack notice when Charlotte went out at night?

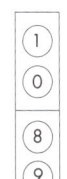

   _____

One day something terrible happened. The shepherd fell over and broke his leg. Jack barked and circled around him, but that didn't help one bit. The shepherd lay in the grass, not knowing what to do.

"Oh dear, oh dear," said the older sheep. "Somebody must go to the farmer's house in the valley and get help."

"Jack should go. He is the only one who knows the way."

"But it is too far. He hardly manages with the herd these days."

"Yes, that's true," said the others, shaking their heads in despair.

6. Why was the shepherd lying in the grass?

    Ⓐ He didn't want to visit the farmer.

    Ⓑ He had broken his leg.

    Ⓒ He wanted to go to sleep.

    Ⓓ He was gazing at the moon.

7. Where did the animals need to go to get help?

    ✎ _____

8. Give **one** reason why Jack was the best one to get help.

    ✎ _____

    Give **one** reason why Jack was NOT the best one to get help.

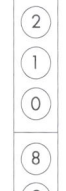

    ✎ _____

Then Charlotte said, "I'll do it. I'll go."

"Charlotte?" muttered the older sheep.

"Out of the question! A sheep has never gone to the valley alone."

The older sheep were beside themselves with worry. But Charlotte couldn't hear them. She had already left to find the right way to the valley.

She bounded over fields, through the stream, and over the mountain.

9. How did the older sheep feel when Charlotte left?

   - Ⓐ happy
   - Ⓑ relieved
   - Ⓒ worried
   - Ⓓ angry

10. Why couldn't Charlotte hear the older sheep?

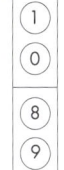

    ✏️ _____

When Charlotte reached the busy road, it was the middle of the night. She stood and watched the traffic.

A truck driver noticed Charlotte and stopped in the road.

"Going to the valley?" he asked. Charlotte nodded.

11. When did Charlotte reach the road?

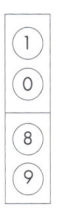

    ✎1 _____

12. What did Charlotte do when she reached the road?

    Ⓐ She walked towards the farmer's house.

    Ⓑ She stood and watched the traffic.

    Ⓒ She tried to cross the road.

    Ⓓ She waved for a truck to stop.

It was so nice to speed along in the truck that Charlotte was almost sorry when they reached the farmer's house.

The farmer was asleep when Charlotte tapped on his window with her nose.

"It's Charlotte," said the farmer, "and she is all alone. Something must be wrong."

13. Why was Charlotte almost sorry to reach the farmer's house?

   Ⓐ She missed the other sheep.

   Ⓑ She would have to wake up the farmer.

   Ⓒ She liked the ride in the truck.

   Ⓓ She was worried about the shepherd.

14. How did the farmer know something was wrong?

   Ⓐ Charlotte was all alone.

   Ⓑ Charlotte told him.

   Ⓒ Charlotte came in a truck.

   Ⓓ Charlotte looked sorry.

Charlotte and the farmer drove on the tractor to find the other sheep. When they arrived, the poor shepherd was still lying in the grass. The farmer took him to the hospital right away.

The shepherd had his leg in a cast for six weeks before he could go back to the sheep. When he returned, he gave Charlotte a big smile. From then on, Charlotte was free to roam as she pleased.

15. What did the farmer and Charlotte do together?

16. How long did the shepherd have a cast on his leg?

17. Why did the shepherd give Charlotte a big smile?

18. Put the events from the story in the correct order. The first one has been done for you.

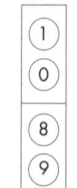

✏️

____ The shepherd goes to the hospital.

____ Charlotte goes to the valley.

_1_ The shepherd needs help.

____ The farmer finds the shepherd.

Scoring Guides for Constructed-response Questions

Brave Charlotte, Item 1

1. Who is Jack?

Purpose: Literary
Process: Focus on and Retrieve Explicitly Stated Information

1 – Acceptable Response

The response indicates that Jack is a/an old sheep dog.

Examples:

old sheep dog

sheep dog

dog

shepherd's dog

0 – Unacceptable Response

The response does not indicate that Jack is an old sheep dog. The response may provide an overly vague description of Jack or describe something that Jack does in the story.

Examples:

sheep

shepherd

animal (Please note that this response is too vague.)

He's the one that takes care of the sheep.

He keeps Charlotte under control.

Non-Response Codes

8 – Not administered. Question misprinted, page missing, or other reason out of student's control.

9 – Blank

Brave Charlotte, Item 2

2. What did Jack try to do with Charlotte?

Purpose: Literary
Process: Focus on and Retrieve Explicitly Stated Information

1 – Acceptable Response

The response indicates that Jack tries to keep Charlotte under control. Please note that responses paraphrasing this idea are considered acceptable.

Examples:

keep Charlotte under control

control

keep her calm

0 – Unacceptable Response

The response does not indicate that Jack tries to keep Charlotte under control.

Examples:

put Charlotte to sleep

Non-Response Codes

8 – Not administered. Question misprinted, page missing, or other reason out of student's control.

9 – Blank

Brave Charlotte, Item 3

3. Give two ways that Charlotte was different from the other sheep.

Purpose: Literary
Process: Interpret and Integrate Ideas and Information

2 – Complete Comprehension

The response provides two text-based ways that Charlotte was different from the other sheep from the list of acceptable responses below. Ways listed on the same line are considered the same idea and cannot be credited separately.

NOTE TO SCORERS: Responses paraphrasing these ideas are considered acceptable as long as the meaning is clear.

Ways that Charlotte was different from other sheep:

She was brave. / She was not shy.

She was leaping around (while other sheep stood by their mothers). / She didn't stand by her mother.

She was ready for adventure.

She jumped over a riverbank and went swimming.

She secretly roamed the countryside at night.

She slipped away to her special place (and gazed at the moon) (while other sheep were sleeping).

She went to save the shepherd. (*Please note that specific actions that were involved in saving the shepherd, such as riding in a truck, are also acceptable.*)

1 – Partial Comprehension

The response provides one text-based way that Charlotte was different from the other sheep from the list of acceptable responses above.

0 – No Comprehension

The response does not provide any text-based way that Charlotte was different from the other sheep.

Examples:

She wasn't scared of Jack. (*Please note that the text does not state that the other sheep are scared of Jack.*)

She was shy.

She was scared.

Non-Response Codes

8 – Not administered. Question misprinted, page missing, or other reason out of student's control.

9 – Blank

Brave Charlotte, Item 5

5. Why didn't Jack notice when Charlotte went out at night?

Purpose: Literary
Process: Make Straightforward Inferences

1 – Acceptable Response

The response indicates that Jack did not notice Charlotte because he could not hear very well.

Examples:

He didn't have very good hearing.

His ears were bad.

He didn't hear her.

0 – Unacceptable Response

The response does not recognize that Jack could not hear very well. The response may indicate that Jack was old, but does not connect this to his lack of hearing.

Examples:

He was asleep.

He was old. (*Please note that this response is too vague to be considered accurate.*)

Non-Response Codes

8 – Not administered. Question misprinted, page missing, or other reason out of student's control.

9 – Blank

Brave Charlotte, Item 7

7. Where did the animals need to go to get help?

Purpose: Literary
Process: Focus on and Retrieve Explicitly Stated Information

1 – Acceptable Response

The response identifies the farmer's house in the valley as the place to go for help.
  Examples:
  the farmer's house

  to the valley

  to the farmer

0 – Unacceptable Response

The response does not identify the farmer's house in the valley as the place to go for help.
  Examples:
  a farm

  to the road (*Please note that this is an intermediate location, not the destination.*)

  to the stream

Non-Response Codes

8 – Not administered. Question misprinted, page missing, or other reason out of student's control.

9 – Blank

Brave Charlotte, Item 8

8. Give one reason why Jack was the best one to get help. Give one reason why Jack was NOT the best one to get help.

Purpose: Literary
Process: Make Straightforward Inferences

2 – Complete Comprehension

The response provides a plausible text-based reason why Jack was the best one to get help AND a reason why Jack was not the best one to get help from the lists below.

Why Jack was the best:

He knew where to go.

He knew how to get to the farmer's house/valley.

Why Jack was NOT the best:

He is too old to go that far.

It was too far for him to travel.

He can't manage the distance.

He needed to stay and watch the sheep.

He's too slow/weak.

He hardly manages with the herd these days.

1 – Partial Comprehension

The response provides a plausible text-based reason why Jack was the best one to get help OR a reason why Jack was not the best one to get help from the lists above.

0 – No Comprehension

The response does not provide a plausible text-based reason for why Jack was the best one to get help or a reason why he was not the best one to get help.

Example:

He was the best because he was the fastest.

Non-Response Codes

8 – Not administered. Question misprinted, page missing, or other reason out of student's control.

9 – Blank

Brave Charlotte, Item 10

10. Why couldn't Charlotte hear the older sheep?

Purpose: Literary
Process: Focus on and Retrieve Explicitly Stated Information

1 – Acceptable Response

The response indicates that Charlotte could not hear the sheep because she had already left to go to the farmer's house.

Examples:

She had already left.

She already was on her way to the farmer's house.

She was too far away.

0 – Unacceptable Response

The response does not indicate that Charlotte had already left to go to the farmer's house.

Example:

She had bad ears.

Non-Response Codes

8 – Not administered. Question misprinted, page missing, or other reason out of student's control.

9 – Blank

Brave Charlotte, Item 11

11. When did Charlotte reach the road?

Purpose: Literary
Process: Focus on and Retrieve Explicitly Stated Information

1 – Acceptable Response

The response identifies the time (middle of the night) that Charlotte reached the road.
Examples:
in the middle of the night

at night

night

0 –Unacceptable Response

The response does not identify the time that Charlotte reached the road.
Examples:
in the middle

when the farmer was sleeping (*Please note that the text does not state that the farmer was asleep when Charlotte reached the road.*)

Non-Response Codes

8 – Not administered. Question misprinted, page missing, or other reason out of student's control.

9 – Blank

Brave Charlotte, Item 15

15. What did the farmer and Charlotte do together?

Purpose: Literary
Process: Focus on and Retrieve Explicitly Stated Information

1 – Acceptable Response

The response indicates that Charlotte and the farmer drove a tractor out to the sheep.

Examples:

drove a tractor out to the sheep

drove

They rode together.

found the sheep

They went to get the shepherd.

0 – Unacceptable Response

The response does not indicate that Charlotte and the farmer drove a tractor out to the sheep. The response may provide an action from the wrong part of the text.

Examples:

They went to the hospital. (*Please note that the farmer did this with the shepherd.*)

They went to the valley. (*Please note that Charlotte did this on her own.*)

They rode in a truck. (*Please note that Charlotte did this earlier in the story.*)

Non-Response Codes

8 – Not administered. Question misprinted, page missing, or other reason out of student's control.

9 – Blank

Brave Charlotte, Item 16

16. How long did the shepherd have a cast on his leg?

Purpose: Literary
Process: Focus on and Retrieve Explicitly Stated Information

1 – Acceptable Response

The response indicates that the shepherd wore the cast for six (6) weeks.

Example:

six weeks

6 weeks

0 – Unacceptable Response

The response does not indicate that the shepherd wore the cast for six weeks.

Example:

six

Non-Response Codes

8 – Not administered. Question misprinted, page missing, or other reason out of student's control.

9 – Blank

Brave Charlotte, Item 17

17. Why did the shepherd give Charlotte a big smile?

Purpose: Literary
Process: Interpret and Integrate Ideas and Information

1 – Acceptable Response

The response indicates that the shepherd smiled at Charlotte because he was grateful to her (for helping him/getting the farmer), or the response may provide a more general indication that the shepherd was proud of Charlotte.

Examples:

She had gone to get the farmer.

She had gone to get help.

He was thankful.

She saved him.

She helped him.

He was proud of her.

because she was brave

0 – Unacceptable Response

The response does not indicate that the shepherd smiled at Charlotte because she had helped him by getting the farmer or because he was proud of her.

Examples:

He liked her.

He was happy.

From then on, Charlotte was free to roam as she pleased.

Non-Response Codes

8 – Not administered. Question misprinted, page missing, or other reason out of student's control.

9 – Blank

Brave Charlotte, Item 18

18. Put the events from the story in the correct order. The first one has been done for you.

    ____ The shepherd goes to the hospital.
    ____ Charlotte goes to the valley.
    _1_ The shepherd needs help.
    ____ The farmer finds the shepherd.

Purpose: Literary
Process: Interpret and Integrate Ideas and Information

1 – Acceptable Response

The response recognizes the order of the events from the story (4, 2, 1, 3).

    _4_ The shepherd goes to the hospital.
    _2_ Charlotte goes to the valley.
    _1_ The shepherd needs help.
    _3_ The farmer finds the shepherd.

0 – Unacceptable Response

The response does not recognize the order of the events from the story.

Non-Response Codes

8 – Not administered. Question misprinted, page missing, or other reason out of student's control.

9 – Blank

PIRLS 2016 FRAMEWORK: C SAMPLE PIRLS LITERACY PASSAGES

Caterpillar to Butterfly

By Deborah Heiligman
Illustrated by Bari Weissman

One day our teacher brought a caterpillar to school in a jar. It was eating green leaves. This tiny caterpillar was going to change into a butterfly. Caterpillars usually turn into butterflies outdoors. But we watched our caterpillar change into a butterfly right in our classroom.

1. What was the caterpillar eating when the teacher first showed it to the children?

   _____

2. Where did the children watch the caterpillar turn into a butterfly?

   _____

Our teacher told us our caterpillar started out as a tiny egg. The mother butterfly laid the egg on a leaf. The mother butterfly chose the leaf of a plant that the caterpillar would eat. When the caterpillar hatched out of the egg, it was hungry. It ate its own eggshell! Then it started to eat green plants right away.

The caterpillar's job was to eat and eat, so it would grow. Each day it got bigger. The caterpillar ate and grew for 12 days.

3. Why did the egg need to be on a leaf?

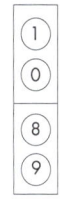

_____

_____

4. What was the first thing the caterpillar did when it hatched?

- Ⓐ chose a leaf
- Ⓑ ate its eggshell
- Ⓒ ate green plants
- Ⓓ laid an egg

Our skin grows with us. But a caterpillar's skin does not grow. When the caterpillar got too big for its skin, the skin split down the back.

The caterpillar crawled right out of its own skin. It had a new skin underneath. This is called shedding. Our caterpillar shed its skin four times. After many days our caterpillar was finished growing. It was almost as big as my little finger.

5. How is a caterpillar's skin different from human skin?

   Ⓐ It does not grow.

   Ⓑ It is too big for the caterpillar.

   Ⓒ It grows for many days.

   Ⓓ A caterpillar can crawl in its skin.

6. Why did the caterpillar need to shed its skin?

   Ⓐ Its skin got smaller.

   Ⓑ It was hungry.

   Ⓒ It got too big for its skin.

   Ⓓ Its skin got too old.

7. How many times did the caterpillar shed its skin?

   _____

8. How big was the caterpillar when it finished growing?

   _____

Then our caterpillar made a special house. First it made a button of silk. It used this button to hang upside down from a twig.

Button of silk

Then it shed its skin for the last time. Instead of a new skin, this time it formed a chrysalis with a hard shell. We watched the chrysalis for a long time.

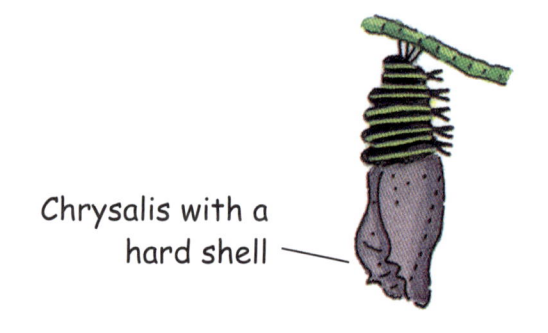

Chrysalis with a hard shell

Every day the shell looked the same. But inside the shell changes were happening.

9. What did the caterpillar use a button of silk for?

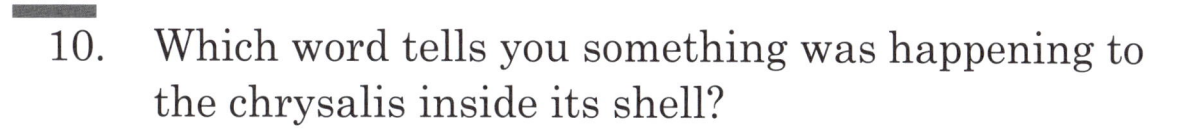

_____

_____

10. Which word tells you something was happening to the chrysalis inside its shell?

   Ⓐ changes

   Ⓑ button

   Ⓒ shed

   Ⓓ watched

We waited and waited. Then, one day, somebody shouted, "Look!" The shell was cracking. It was a butterfly! Our butterfly was damp and crumpled. It hung on to the shell while its wings flapped. This pumped blood into its wings. The wings stretched out and dried. Soon our butterfly was ready to fly.

11. What came out of the shell?

    Ⓐ a green leaf

    Ⓑ a new caterpillar

    Ⓒ a tiny egg

    Ⓓ a butterfly

12. How did the butterfly pump blood into its wings?

    Ⓐ by drying them

    Ⓑ by flapping them

    Ⓒ by stretching them

    Ⓓ by crumpling them

Our butterfly could not stay in the jar. It needed to be outside with flowers and grass and trees. We watched our butterfly land on a flower. It sipped the flower's nectar through a long, coiled tube. Maybe it was a female butterfly. Maybe someday she would lay an egg on a leaf.

13. Why couldn't the butterfly stay in the jar?

   Ⓐ They did not want to watch it anymore.

   Ⓑ They wanted another caterpillar.

   Ⓒ It was too big for the jar.

   Ⓓ It needed to be free outdoors.

14. How did the butterfly get the flower nectar?

   Ⓐ ate flowers and grass

   Ⓑ chewed green leaves

   Ⓒ sipped through a tube

   Ⓓ pumped its wings

15. Put what happens to a caterpillar as it changes into a butterfly in the correct order. The first one has been done for you.

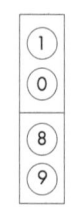

　　　____　The caterpillar forms a hard shell.

　　　_1_　The caterpillar eats and grows.

　　　____　The butterfly flaps its wings.

　　　____　The shell of the chrysalis cracks.

16. Think about the whole article. Why do you think the teacher brought the caterpillar into the classroom?

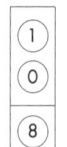

_____
_____
_____

Scoring Guides for Constructed-response Questions

Caterpillar to Butterfly, Item 1

1. What was the caterpillar eating when the teacher first showed it to the children?

Purpose: Acquire and Use Information
Process: Focus on and Retrieve Explicitly Stated Information

1 – Acceptable Response

The response indicates that the caterpillar was eating leaves.

Examples:

The caterpillar was eating green leaves.

leaves

plants

0 – Unacceptable Response

The response does not indicate that the caterpillar was eating leaves.

Example:

food

Non-Response Codes

8 – Not administered. Question misprinted, page missing, or other reason out of student's control.

9 – Blank

Caterpillar to Butterfly, Item 2

2. Where did the children watch the caterpillar turn into a butterfly?

Purpose: Acquire and Use Information
Process: Focus on and Retrieve Explicitly Stated Information

1 – Acceptable Response

The response indicates that the children watched the caterpillar change in a jar or, more generally, in their classroom/at school.

Examples:

in a jar

in the class

at school

0 – Unacceptable Response

The response does not indicate that the children watched the caterpillar change in a jar or in their classroom.

Examples:

outside

on a leaf

Non-Response Codes

8 – Not administered. Question misprinted, page missing, or other reason out of student's control.

9 – Blank

Caterpillar to Butterfly, Item 3

3. Why did the egg need to be on a leaf?

Purpose: Acquire and Use Information
Process: Interpret and Integrate Ideas and Information

1 – Acceptable Response

The response indicates that the egg was laid on a green leaf so that the caterpillar would have food to eat (as soon as it hatched).

Examples:

so it would have food
The caterpillar could eat it.
The caterpillar would be hungry.
to eat it

0 – Unacceptable Response

The response does not indicate that the egg was laid on a leaf so that the caterpillar would have food to eat when it hatched.

Examples:

so the butterfly could eat it
so it could grow
to eat (*Please note that this response is too vague.*)

Non-Response Codes

8 – Not administered. Question misprinted, page missing, or other reason out of student's control.

9 – Blank

Caterpillar to Butterfly, Item 7

7. How many times did the caterpillar shed its skin?

Purpose: Acquire and Use Information
Process: Focus on and Retrieve Explicitly Stated Information

1 – Acceptable Response

The response indicates that the caterpillar sheds its skin four (4) times.

Examples:

four times
four
4

0 – Unacceptable Response

The response does not recognize that the caterpillar sheds four times.

Examples:

four days
five times

Non-Response Codes

8 – Not administered. Question misprinted, page missing, or other reason out of student's control.

9 – Blank

Caterpillar to Butterfly, Item 8

8. How big was the caterpillar when it finished growing?

Purpose: Acquire and Use Information
Process: Focus on and Retrieve Explicitly Stated Information

1 – Acceptable Response

The response indicates that the caterpillar was the size of a little finger when it finished growing.

Examples:

It was as big as my little finger.
the size of a boy's little finger
finger

0 – Unacceptable Response

The response does not indicate that the caterpillar was the size of a little finger when it finished growing.

Examples:

as big as a hand
big
It was small.

Non-Response Codes

8 – Not administered. Question misprinted, page missing, or other reason out of student's control.

9 – Blank

Caterpillar to Butterfly, Item 9

9. What did the caterpillar use a button of silk for?

Purpose: Acquire and Use Information
Process: Focus on and Retrieve Explicitly Stated Information

1 – Acceptable Response

The response recognizes that the caterpillar uses a button of silk to hang (from a twig).

Examples:

to hang upside down
to hang
hang from a twig

0 – Unacceptable Response

The response does not recognize that the caterpillar uses a button of silk to hang from a twig. The response may repeat words from the question.

Examples:

to eat
to make a house

Non-Response Codes

8 – Not administered. Question misprinted, page missing, or other reason out of student's control.

9 – Blank

Caterpillar to Butterfly, Item 15

15. Put what happens to a caterpillar as it changes into a butterfly in the correct order. The first one has been done for you.

 ____ The caterpillar forms a hard shell.
 _1_ The caterpillar eats and grows.
 ____ The butterfly flaps its wings.
 ____ The shell of the chrysalis cracks.

Purpose: Acquire and Use Information
Process: Interpret and Integrate Information and Ideas

1 – Acceptable Response

The response provides the correct order of the events in the article (2, 1, 4, 3).

 _2_ The caterpillar forms a hard shell.
 _1_ The caterpillar eats and grows.
 _4_ The butterfly flaps its wings.
 _3_ The shell of the chrysalis cracks.

0 – Unacceptable Response

The response does not provide the correct order of the events in the article.

Non-Response Codes

8 – Not administered. Question misprinted, page missing, or other reason out of student's control.

9 – Blank

Caterpillar to Butterfly, Item 16

16. Think about the whole article. Why do you think the teacher brought the caterpillar into the classroom?

Purpose: Acquire and Use Information
Process: Examine and Evaluate Content, Language, and Textual Elements

1 – Acceptable Response

The response recognizes that the teacher brought the caterpillar into class for students to see it change/grow (into a butterfly).

Examples:

- to see it change into a butterfly
- to learn how butterflies form
- so they could see it change
- because she wanted them to see it grow

OR, the response may recognize that the teacher wanted students to learn about butterflies, without explicitly mentioning change from a caterpillar.

Examples:

- to learn about butterflies
- to show how a butterfly works

OR, the response may indicate a general understanding that the teacher wanted students to learn about the caterpillar's cycle of life without explicitly mentioning its change into a butterfly.

Examples:

- to learn about the cycle of life
- to learn about the caterpillar's cycle
- to learn how a caterpillar's life begins and ends

0 – Unacceptable Response

The response provides only a vague understanding of the reason the teacher brought the caterpillar into class, or may provide an inaccurate description of why the teacher brought in the caterpillar.

Examples:

- to learn about caterpillars
- to watch it eat
- to learn about nature
- It was neat.

Non-Response Codes

8 – Not administered. Question misprinted, page missing, or other reason out of student's control.

9 – Blank